One Man, One Cross

ONE MAN
ONE CROSS

A Spiritual Journey

BILLY TURNER

GRAYSTONE PUBLISHING
"Where ideas are boundless and the possibilities unlimited."

© 2000 Billy Turner. All rights reserved.
No portion of this book may be reproduced or used in any form, or by any means, without prior written permission of the publisher.

GRAYSTONE PUBLISHING
"Where ideas are boundless and the possibilities unlimited."
Madison, Mississippi

First printing in May, 2000
10 9 8 7 6 5 4 3 2 1

Manufactured in the United States of America

Publisher's Cataloging-in-Publication
(Provided by Quality Books, Inc.)

Turner, Billy V.
    One man, one cross : a spiritual journey / Billy Turner. -- 1st ed.
    p. cm.
    LCCN: 00-103108
    ISBN: 0-9663078-7-9

    1. Turner, Billy V.--Religion. 2. Spiritual journals. 3. Alcoholism--Religious aspects--Christianity. I. Title.

BL73.T87A3 2000   270.092
                    QBI00-408

Dedication

This book is dedicated to all those who are seekers, those who have tried to fill the holes in their lives with alcohol, drugs or anything the world has to offer, and have found the better way.

I wish to thank Judi McLain and Graystone Publishing for their efforts when no one else saw the possibility that this book might help someone.

I dedicate it also to The Bible Cruisers, to Gretna United Methodist Church where I was taken in and given a home, to Roger and Cathy who started this whole journal thing and to my mother, Deloris. I thank Tim Ellerbee for giving me a chance at sobriety.

But most importantly, this book is dedicated to my family, Mary, Jason, Shanna and Carrie, for their patience and love.

All glory to God for His son's deliverance of the lost.

May God bless you and keep you, as He certainly has me.

Preface

*"For I know the plans I have for you," declares the Lord,
"plans to prosper you and not to harm you; plans to give
you hope and a future.
"Then you will call on me and come and pray to me, and
I will listen to you.
"You will seek me and find me when you seek me with all
your heart."*
—Jeremiah 29: 11-13*

* *Bible quotations in this book are from the New International Version.*

It's funny how things turn out.

I knew I had a drinking problem, knew my life wasn't turning out the way I had hoped it would, knew I wanted to find happiness somehow, some way.

But I didn't mean to go in search of, much less find, God.

In no way am I proud, for to take pride in what God has accomplished in me during the past year would be to maintain guilt over what I did wrong for many years. I now know that some of what happened to me wasn't my fault. But I've learned forgiveness. It's not something I can reach into my back pocket and pull out on demand yet. But it's a goal that my friend has set for me. And as I grow, climbing fingernail by fingernail up the slippery slope of life, I do find that forgiveness is easier to call on.

Let's go back to where I was and follow what happened to a lost sinner. The apostle Paul tried on a daily basis to be like

Christ. I try to be like Paul. I don't suggest you be like me. But if your problems in any way resemble mine, I can take you through a bit of the pain, a bit of the struggle. And maybe we'll learn together. Know only that you are not alone. We're in this together.

Let's start at the beginning.

✦ ✦ ✦

The pain I've always felt, what I'm told I felt anyway, came originally from isolation. I felt deserted by some people I still haven't met. I know my birth mother's name, now. But I have not looked for her.

Years passed, and I made more and more of a mess of myself. In secret. Always in secret. At least I thought. I never let anyone close. My significant others and children learned to live with the pain every bit as much as I did.

I've learned in my year of spiritual discovery that I am, among other things, an adult child of an alcoholic, a codependent, an alcoholic, a sinner, a searcher, a depressed divorcé, a spendaholic, an abused child, a victim, an abuser, and an egotist. I didn't get a blessing either from my birth father or from my adopted father.

I'm from a blue-collar household, from rural Mississippi. I never graduated from college and didn't have many advantages.

I was overweight, with high cholesterol and blood pressure. I developed an ulcer at eighteen. I should have bought stock in Rolaids at twenty, because every meal brought tremendous indigestion, often pain. I was out of shape, out of ideas, and about out of time.

Those companies I didn't owe money to should have been ashamed. Their advertising departments must have been terrible. If I had heard of them, I owed them. American Express and I were on a first-name basis. Maybe you know the routine. "Billy, when can we expect a payment?" "Oh, any day now,

Martha. That loan I took out with Avco should be coming in at any moment."

Throw me in a brown paper bag with millions of others throughout this world that God never intended, shake us and pour us out, and you couldn't tell us apart.

But there is a way to start over. To be born again. To start at the point where I fell and to be given another chance. Because (here comes the most important part) "those who are led by the Spirit of God are sons of God." (1 Romans 8: 13)

Now, that revelation, that understanding didn't come overnight. Or even over a series of many nights. When I was considering what to do with this wasted life, all I really saw of myself was that I was in my forty-second year, that I wasn't happy with my past or my present, and that the future looked unfriendly.

It wasn't the kids. It wasn't my wife. It wasn't even the job. However, I can't say I was satisfied with any of the three all the time. I was also judgmental. Everyone else had something wrong with him or her.

I didn't dislike myself, totally. There were bits and pieces of whatever is me that I liked. But the parts I didn't like caused me to drink. I looked for refuge and found it at the bottom of a beer can or fifth of Canadian Club.

The kids and Mary, my present wife, seemed to be happy. But then, what does a selfish person notice? Their smiles hid little hurts and embarrassments I knew nothing about. Their hugs masked the questions about how Dad was acting. I never stopped long enough to consider how my drinking and my unhappiness would affect them. I could only handle one child at a time—and I was the child. I certainly wasn't handling it properly.

But I didn't know that.

I wasn't trying to be unhappy. No one does.

People see that their lives aren't what they meant them to be, what God meant them to be, but don't know how to get out of the rut, out of the meaninglessness. Or, if someone is like me, and believes that there has to be something more, then somehow we begin to claw, scrape, and struggle out of a self-made gutter. Then, and only then, we discovered that we cannot get out by our own power.

I acknowledge that my situation was of my own making. In the beginning, quite willingly, I created havoc.

But I didn't pick that way to live. Not by a long shot. I tried religion early, upon demand of my adoptive mother. I sang the solos, even preached, formed a gospel band. And slid away to find myself in the world.

I had success, as I knew it to be. I had a good career. I made plenty of money working in states where people lived far below the poverty level in alarming numbers.

Some of what I was feeling, admittedly, had to do with my age. For the first time, I could see death approaching like car lights ascending a lonely winding mountain road. Death was out there, somewhere, and with my father's rather recent demise, it was entering my mind more and more often.

Was this all there was?

Was this all I could be?

Twenty years of work, and all it got me was bored. Life's meaning was packing up and moving away.

I thought that if I could stop drinking, get control of myself, maybe start a bank account, these problems would be yesterday's news. I thought I would be yelling at the kids, "Hey, remember when I used to drink?" from the veranda of our mansion.

I had little idea of where to go for help, or even if there actually was any help to be found. Had there been anyone quite like me to come down the pike in all of time?

I had tried to stop drinking so many times it was almost a scripted scenario. But getting the courage to go ask someone for help just wasn't in me.

This book is the story of the road I traveled to answer all these questions, to wash myself clean of the dirt I had wiped on myself for all those years. It wasn't a smooth road, as the excerpts from the year-long diary show.

There were days when the urge to quit everything and go back to what I had come to know as normal was so strong that I just wanted to cry. Some days I acted on those urges, and the tears flowed. At times I cried out for help. At times I just cried.

There were also times of pure ecstasy, when the grace God gives to us if we will accept it washed over, around, and through me.

You never know where you're going. I looked for sobriety and found God. I looked for a way to take control of my life and found that the only way was to surrender the steering wheel to Jesus. I found books that helped, people that helped, times that helped, meetings, steps, prayers, and methods that helped. Each played a part in helping me find meaning for my life, and where there was misery there is gratitude.

The road goes on. The spiritual journey continues. The old car engine is still humming. If God be willing, this will never end. But I want to make sure that all who are reading this understand that they are not alone. There is absolutely no reason to feel alone. There's a strong chance that whatever anyone is feeling guilty about, I've done.

I have found meaning, grace, and salvation for my life, for my soul. Life is better, not perfect, but remarkably better.

I'm not insisting that everyone take the same journey I took, although I think the experiences will be somewhat familiar to anyone who had any of the problems I had and have. Sometimes, as the members of Alcoholics Anonymous will tell you, you have to reach "a bottom" before you can begin the crawl back to the top. Christians will tell you that your heart must be broken in the right place for the healing to begin.

I only know that God has a plan for each of us, and I believe that there has been a spiritual reason for all I've gone through. I believe that with all my being.

God's grace became my desire. And it became apparent that

the way to grace was through faith. My faith was in Jesus Christ, the only way to the Father, a Father not of my own choosing. That is the 13th step, the step beyond sobriety. The purpose is sobriety, but the result I pray, is salvation.

You can't over-seek this help. You can't overreach You can't work your way out of trouble. You can't hunger and thirst for help too much or you won't be able to do this at all.

You don't sober up or grow spiritually or do anything on your own.

If you'll listen for a while, maybe curl up on a comfortable chair in the quiet, away from the tinkling ice of a mixed drink or the banging cymbals of the latest of your life's problems, you'll find what I have been given.

It's not love until you give it away.

And I intend to give as much as this vessel can pour out.

Stick a helpless, shaking hand out, palms uplifted and open, holding on to nothing, and ask for help for just a second, just a mere fraction of the time it takes to read this sentence. I promise that the road I traveled will begin to intersect with your journey.

We will begin the search, together, for happiness. I'll show you my conclusions, and you can make your own about a journal I kept for the first year of my journey.

And if we can't find happiness, at least we'll try to find a peace that surpasses all understanding.

I have.

PART ONE

CHAPTER 1

Micky Mantle and Garth Brooks

The sons of Noah who came out of the ark were Shem, Ham and Japheth. (Ham was the father of Canaan.) These were the three sons of Noah, and from them came the people who were scattered all over the earth. Noah, a man of the soil, proceeded to plant a vineyard. When he drank some of his wine, he became drunk and lay uncovered inside his tent. Ham, the father of Canaan, saw his father's nakedness and told his two brothers outside. But Shem and Japheth took a garment and laid it across their shoulders; then they walked in backward and covered their father's nakedness. Their faces were turned the other way so that they could not see their father's nakedness.
—Genesis 9: 18-23

Spending time during the summer in New Orleans is like being just outside the gates of hell. You may not be in the hottest part of the world, but you're close enough to smell the sulfur.

You can imagine clean, cool air being breathed somewhere in this country. But in the Crescent City, the air is so thick that you can part it with a comb. The heat is constant, unrelenting, unless it is the monsoon season, which apparently hits every couple of years. Then the temperature dips as the city slowly sinks below a line of brown, trashy water, and the pumps don't work.

It was during such a summer, in the year of my forty-second birthday, that my spirit, so tired, worn, and drunk out, came crashing down.

Even now, I don't really understand what was different about that summer, that birthday. Maybe it was God's time for me. Maybe it was just more than I could keep on trying to manage, however badly.

I tend to blame Mickey and Garth.

One thing has to be understood about my family: we're sports-minded, mainly because of me. I've been in the sports business since I was eight. That was when I argued with my mom about those funny-looking socks baseball players wear, the ones with the holes in the bottoms that form stirrups, saying that nothing was supposed to be worn underneath.

The holes were to keep the feet cool. I knew this because a friend had told me. And what better authority could one have than a fellow eight-year-old who could throw a baseball from the mound all the way to home plate without so much as one bounce?

That began both my baseball career and my refusal to be wrong. Neither would serve me very well.

But from playing peewee baseball, as we called it, to high school baseball, football, and basketball, I developed a pure love for sport that guided me toward a career beginning with my writing for the local newspaper when I was seventeen.

Now, about never being wrong. That notion served me up until the moment I realized I had a drinking problem and could not possibly do anything about it by myself.

When did that decision come?

Slowly, over years, through my father's death and the deaths of many in his family, through a divorce almost directly attributable to alcohol. There is something shattering about seeing your father die as slowly as grass grows, watching such life sucked out of him that he is dressed in diapers while his body, not his mind, hangs on by the width of his fingernails.

Right up until Mickey's death.

Let's go back to the beginning, when I undertook to become the Lord of the Drink. We've got to understand what leads one to pick up that drink for reasons other than refreshment. We need to understand what turns this normal occurrence into a disease. For that is what I learned I had. On top of everything else, now I had a disease. And I really thought I just had to get rid of the drinking and life would sort of fix itself. Drinking was my only problem, I thought at the time.

And that was the biggest problem of all.

But I'm getting ahead of the story, like a man who knows the answer and just can't wait to tell it. That's me, too.

I took my first drink, Budweiser from a tall can, when I was sixteen. Actually, that's not right. That was my first real drink. There were moments before that when someone deemed it cute to give the kid a sip of beer or some whiskey.

One Christmas in New York when I was fifteen, some relatives gave me shots of rye whiskey. It was a terribly cold night, certainly frigid by the standards I knew. I learned later, after a sixteen-block walk to Lincoln Center, that it was unusually cold even for New York. My cousin, the tour guide I would never believe again, kept saying we would stop for hot chocolate.

But no cafes were open down the stretch of windblown streets where we were walking. Finally, we came to an apartment where someone had a friendly smile for my cousin and then produced little glasses filled with an amber liquid.

It burned going down like the gulp of Dad's black coffee he occasionally gave me. But it bottomed with a glow I had never experienced before, a warmth I couldn't imagine, coming from a single finger of whiskey.

When I was sixteen, however, it got a little more serious.

Rickey, Stanley, and Sonny—my lifelong friends I seldom talk to now—and I were presented an opportunity. My mom and dad were gone, somewhere, apparently for the night. The details are lost in the haze of time. But the drunk's first drink is never forgotten, as I later learned.

And, Lord help me, I remember the absolute coldness of that drink. I remember the bitterness at first. I remember the smell. I remember the laughter as we poured down the brew. We were young, invincible, probably what passed for normal. We had lied about our ages, bought a six-pack, and scrambled out of town in the yellow 1969 Mercury Comet I affectionately called Mokey Bear.

I remember the quiet of the night. A breeze, the kind you can really only find deep in rural America, the kind that lifts branches and gently puts them back in place, cooled us as we laughed loudly. We knocked back first sips, then slugs. It became easier to swallow with each tip of the can.

The evening was dark, as all nights are in the country. (The biggest difference between inner-cities and rural America isn't the availability of drugs or the crime. The biggest difference is the quiet, the darkness, the stillness versus the silly pace that grabs people in the city.) That night, as we celebrated belonging, to each other and to the adulthood roaring at us, with the splash of foamy beer and tears of laughter, I thought I would never be happier. The beer took away all reservations I had about myself. It lifted; it pulled. It was my first step toward using alcohol as a crutch.

I thought the laughter came from the beer. I thought it made me more of a real person than I could be. All you had to do was turn it up and you belonged. I was like my friends, lying under a full moon on pasture hay. We were free to holler till our chests hurt.

The difference between the others and myself, as with alcoholics everywhere, is that it was the beginning of a road that almost killed me.

You hear a lot about the ravages of alcohol. You see the bums on the street, asking, begging, for just a dollar or a moment of our precious time. And we hurry past, because these people are so lowly. But I passed quite nicely through job after job, promotion after promotion, award after award. And I spent most of a fifteen-year period either drunk or on the back end of a hangover.

If anyone had stopped to offer me a hand, told me that it was time to shape up or get out, maybe I wouldn't have needed Garth and Mickey. But I doubt that things would have gone differently.

According to a theory I have—well, maybe it's not mine, but I'll pass it along as if it were—God has a plan for each of us. I know that there was nothing particularly different about my forty-second summer. Except that I found help. And I don't drink anymore, though I have a predisposition to drink that you wouldn't believe unless you have the same.

It was time. It was past time.

✦ ✦ ✦

God speaks to us in so many ways. As I've mentioned, He spoke to me through the lack of a base hit, through Garth Brooks, and through Mickey Mantle.

I was coaching, as an assistant, a youth league softball team that summer. My daughter Shanna was fourteen. She is a beautiful teenager, with blonde hair curled by permanent (and if they're permanent, why do I have to pay to keep doing it again?). She has blue eyes as deep as ocean pools. She has a laugh that I would pay to hear, and a smile that melts me. And she can hit, field, throw, run, and hit with occasional power.

There's not much more a father could want in a child. (I guess if she would read a book between presidential elections, just one book, I would die a contented man.) She helped me more than you can imagine—by failing. She was the first step in my hitting bottom, in reaching the breaking point that is necessary for you to find out if God can help you.

To explain, I need to go back to the year before that first drink: it was the best summer anyone could ever have had.

✦ ✦ ✦

I am fifteen, or at least playing as a fifteen-year-old. The age cutoff for baseball is August 1, and my birthday is July 27. Every year, from the age of eight until I finished at sixteen, I played as if I were a year older. So when I was fourteen, I played as a fifteen-year-old. The season was well over before I turned fifteen.

Just another strike against me.

That year, the team I am playing for, full of lifelong friends who have always been teammates, strikes gold. We win all eighteen of our games. It is the summer of 1968, the year of the pitcher in major league baseball. Bob Gibson's 1.12 ERA would never be topped. Denny McClain wins thirty-one games.

And in Ponta, Mississippi, Northeast Lauderdale's Babe Ruth team wins all its games.

We're a ragtag bunch. Some power. Some speed. Some left-handed pitching that dominates. We have the absolute time of our lives, constantly joking and laughing. Constantly winning. It's a summer of friendships, of late-night telephone calls to talk baseball, of listening to Creedence Clearwater Revival. Elsewhere, it's a summer of love. For us, it's a summer of fun.

✦ ✦ ✦

Unfortunately, all of the life that followed would be measured against that summer. I played high school baseball and recreational softball, coached a Little League boys' team, and coached Shanna's teams from the time she was eight. Nothing would come.

Winning every game was part of it, but it was also about

being absolutely free, full of friendship and joy. No job. No worries. Get up late in the morning and think about either practice or a game. Although we trailed in almost every game that summer, we always found ways to win.

When Shanna was twelve, she made all-stars, and her team went into the unbeaten game of the double-elimination bracket. I told her the story about that summer for the first time. I pleaded with her to take this game seriously, do whatever it took to play her best this one night, this one game. I told her that winning this tournament could create memories that would last her forever.

They lost.

It was always that way. No victory in a national newspaper contest made a difference to me. I couldn't find ways to accept congratulations. There was always something wrong with the praise. No victory in our little softball games meant much, because we never won a championship. Shanna played well, was always the leading hitter on her team. She was happy, healthy, and a wonderful child.

But she wasn't providing the victory I thought I needed. Her teams always found a way to lose.

In major league baseball, I root for the Atlanta Braves, with passion. The World Series in 1991 almost killed me. I was depressed for a month. The Braves lost the seventh game of the series, 1-0. Somehow, that was me, losing again. Always losing.

My life, as I saw it, was one of coming close to achievement, with something always keeping me from it. I realize that letting the accomplishments of a youth league team or of a major league team that I have nothing to do with affect my demeanor is crazy. I'm sorry. Asking for forgiveness when you have so much guilt becomes quite easy.

Then came the summer when my journey began.

✦ ✦ ✦

It is early June and the last game of the season. We have tied one game, but lost none. We are to play the team resting a half game ahead of us. Shanna is the second-leading hitter on the team. She'd had a marvelous softball season, as had the team.

It comes down to one game. One moment for glory. We are playing the team that always beats us, always wins the league. We are tied, with minutes left in the game, when a girl doubles with one out.

The next girl singles, but somehow we hold our runner at third.

Shanna is up next. All those hours of practice, of throwing her balls as sweat poured off us, were for this very minute. I know it. I smile inside and out. This is the moment when I will return to 1968, wipe away the crud that has grown around my life, like so much rust on an iron swing.

The brilliant New Orleans sun pours down on us, reflecting off the red-clay infield. Shanna, wearing a green shirt with Terrytown stitched in yellow across the front and gray pants with green striping, stands in the batter's box, carrying my hopes, my dreams.

A forty-one year-old man, a professional, a guy who has covered Super Bowls and College World Series games, who has written columns for newspapers across the South and even one out West, is depending on a fourteen-year-old girl to provide meaning for his life.

And I don't think this is strange, at the time.

✦ ✦ ✦

The hit that I was so sure would happen, forcing in the winning run, making us the regular-season champions, giving Shanna her first championship team, never happened.

She struck out. The second time all season she hadn't at least put the bat on the ball. A grounder to the right side of the infield would have won it. A fly ball to the outfield would have won it.

And she struck out.

I stood stunned in the first-base coaching box. Our cleanup hitter grounded out to first on the next pitch of the game. We went to extra innings and were bombed 11-4.

Another opportunity lost. And you just don't get them back, I told myself; it's not like you'll play forever.

And I stepped over the line.

I brooded about that strikeout for weeks. I never said a word. But I drank more and more. What had been three or four six- packs a week turned into six-packs every night. Sometimes there were twelve beers involved. I explained that twelve-packs were cheaper to buy than six-packs. I would split them into two nights, I told Mary. But I didn't. The twelve-packs would go in a single night as the summer rushed along.

Shanna made all-stars again. They practiced almost every night before winning the district tournament. That should have made me feel better. But I had nothing to do with that team. So her championship team of all-stars did not reflect on me at all. I had lost all reason.

Every night as we returned from practice or a game, we would stop at a convenience store and buy Carrie, my youngest child, some candy, Shanna a sports drink, and a six- or twelve-pack of Budweiser.

I didn't miss a day of work or even go in late. I had had years of experience in hiding hangovers. But this was wearing me thin. I felt terrible, really. I had trouble getting started in the morning and arrived home late in the evening drained of emotion and strength. I began the day with headaches and ended it with headaches. I found little to look forward to at work. It was a struggle to care about my vocation.

In the middle of July, for reasons only God knows, I bought a Garth Brooks tape. I am no fan of country music. It was, in fact, the first country music cassette I had ever purchased.

And on that tape was a song titled "I'm Much Too Young to Feel This Damn Old." It was just a song, like the eleven others on that album. But something about it made me start to think, to reflect on where my life had been and where it was going. And it led me back to thinking about Mickey Mantle.

On June 7, 1995, Mantle, perhaps the most talented baseball player I was lucky enough to see while I was growing up (he also played on the only televised team I saw as a kid, since CBS owned the New York Yankees and broadcast their games on a weekly basis), was diagnosed as having liver cancer. Without a transplant, he would die.

He got one, just two days later. But his prognosis was still dire. With a face drawn tight by the surgery and the cancer, the Mick spoke at a press conference just days later. He said that God had blessed him with so much talent and he'd misused it for years.

That stuck me somewhere in the back of my alcohol-ravaged brain.

When your heroes prove to be mortal, when they contract the same disease that killed your own father, when they have what may be affecting you, you relate. Mickey had wanted to fit in. He'd come from Oklahoma a good kid and left New York as an alcoholic. The stories about the drinking were funny back then, in the late 1950s and early 1960s. As Mickey told us about how he wished he'd gotten help much earlier, how things would have been different, he spoke to me.

All these things were rolling around in my head that summer of my forty-second birthday. One day I was sitting at work, feeling burned out, drunked out. The personnel department had sent all managers a little desk calendar with the number of a referral program in case we suspected any of our employees of having a problem. That afternoon I drew the calendar out of a manila envelope, read the information contained in the packet, and went outside to light a Kool and think it over.

And on July 23, Carrie's ninth birthday, I decided I needed help. I just didn't want to die like Dad, like Mickey was dying, without having really lived.

There had to be more.

I didn't really believe anyone could help me, but I knew I had to try. I'd give it everything I had, try to quit drinking, try to make something really special out of my life, try to be a better father and husband.

And when I failed, no one could say I hadn't tried.

That made me feel better.

CHAPTER 2

This Bud's Not For You

"It is not for kings," Lemuel —
not for kings to drink wine,
not for rulers to crave beer,
lest they drink and forget what the law decrees,
and deprive all the oppressed of their rights,
Give beer to those who are perishing,
wine to those who are in anguish;
let them drink and forget their poverty
and remember their misery no more.
—Proverbs 31: 4-7

The twenty-seventh day of July dawned bright, hot, and clear. It was my forty-second birthday. A Thursday. I had taken the day off, as far as my boss knew, to celebrate. Mary and I were the only ones who knew the true reason for my not going in. We'd even sent the kids to my mother's house. This was to be my time. My moment. My agony.

It was hard for me even to make the appointment, to pick up the phone and call. I had asked Mary do it once before, but I hadn't followed through. As I've said, I had "tried to quit." That was what I had called trying—having the wife call for an appointment because I was too ashamed to even talk to a receptionist.

On this particular morning I called at 9:30, having chugged down a pot of coffee and smoked nearly a pack of Kools, to ask directions. I guess I was hoping someone would talk me out of going."Well, Mr. Turner, we've decided from listening to your voice that you really don't need help. You're fine. This little thing with drinking is common. Just slow down, and you'll be fine. The pain you feel? That will go away by the next birthday. The kids? Oh, they'll be fine. It's just a temporary thing. Everyone goes through it. Studies show that male adults need to have their beer as an outlet, given life's stresses. Hey, you know the truth: life's a pressure cooker, and you're a green bean."

But all they gave me was directions.

The appointment was for 1 p.m. Mary and I talked all morning. I told her every reason I could imagine for why I drank, why I felt I needed to quit. I wasn't talking to her, really. I was talking to myself. Building courage. I was the football coach and the player. The coach spoke, tried to motivate, pump up the player. The player saw only how big the other team's players were. I'd played this team before. And always lost. Always.

There was the first time I told the kids I was an alcoholic. I learned a lot about denial in treatment over the next three weeks, but I never really denied it outwardly. My denial was more an acceptance of the inevitable. Dad was a drunk. I was a drunk. Clean, unquestionable.

✦ ✦ ✦

We're at a game of the local minor league baseball club. I've taken Shanna, Jason (my son from the first marriage), Carrie, and Mary to the ball game. For them, it is an opportunity for autographs and souvenirs. Mary likes going somewhere as a family, getting away from the house and into the open air. Somewhere inside, that still is true for me as well. I love the game. The simple rules, the strategy. I love passing along moments, moves, and memories to the kids. I want them to love it with the same unending passion I have.

But actually, the game is an opportunity to drink cold beer. I drink a lot. Cup after large cup. I love draft beer more than I love the game. Mary is my designated driver. The keeper of the keys. So I use the opportunity to enjoy myself. She'd so slowed my drinking, in my mind anyway, that ball games were an opportunity to kick back. This wasn't drinking to ease any pain, to get over a lost opportunity at work, to forget any bill. This was pleasure, the old pleasure I had always felt when the cold beer or icy drink swam down my throat.

I drink them cold, straight from the tap, going slow as they warm in the summer heat, perspiration forming on the souvenir twenty-ounce cup like dew on a fall morning. Later, I drink them cold, going fast so they stay cold. I've always found it odd that a drunk can keep up with the number of drinks he or she has right up until that moment when the switch is thrown and all inhibition goes. I have eight of the big boys before I lose track. I do know that I pulled out the credit card and bought souvenirs at the stand when the money began to run out. The beer fellow wouldn't take credit, so, to preserve the cash, I switched to plastic at the souvenir stand. I don't want the kids to miss out on this fun.

At home, I am barely conscious, barely able to walk. I am a living embarrassment for Mary and the kids. I take Jason and Shanna into Carrie's room and, since I am always able to talk straight and with courage when I am drinking, I tell them that ol' Dad has a problem with the beer. And that I will be getting help soon. Things will get better. I cry, hug them, drunkenly figuring I have explained away all the hurt and embarrassment. What must they think of me? Do they want to imitate me, for God's sake? Do they dislike what I've become? Do they envy me the freedom to do as I want, much as I did my own father? Is the reason Shanna seldom invites friends over her fear that I will do this?

✦ ✦ ✦

That was two years before the July date with destiny.

Drunks always come up with a reason to keep themselves from getting help. They can handle it, they tell their loved ones when they sober up the next day. Until the next drink. They point out that they are the ones who work, who bring in the pay, who keep the household going. They are the ones who know about alcohol. Mary didn't even drink. What could she possibly know about growing up with a drunk? About drinking? I knew there were times when I got drunk, I wasn't stupid. I just hadn't had a meal before the game, or before the company function, or before the televised Atlanta Braves game.

As years passed, however, I began to skip the meals on purpose, so the buzz, the feeling that a drunk can't relate, would come more quickly.

I left for the referral service at noon. Among many other things, I am always early. That may be another problem I have. But that one would have to wait.

I wasn't at all sure where I was going, and I wanted to make a good impression. If I was going to be an alcoholic, admitting to it freely before someone I had never met, I was at least going to be the best one they'd ever seen.

With just a bit of trouble, I found the building. Even found parking. My God. It wasn't a building unto itself. It was an office building. The service was just one of the offices. A rental, for heaven's sake.

✦ ✦ ✦

Step One: I have a last smoke. The condemned always gets one, doesn't he?

Step Two: I take a quick look around, then force myself through a public entry and across a lobby. A barbershop, a finance company (that makes me feel at home), and a florist are among the shops there. I walk quickly, looking as little as I can to the left or right. I don't want to be recognized later.

Step three: Casually, I look up at the black slate with white plastic office numbers. I try to make sure that no one can see me looking under "H." Office number 404.

Step four: As I am about to enter the elevator alone, a young lady steps out of the hallway just off the elevator entrance and, sticking a hand out to catch the shutting doors, walks on with me. I watch her hit the 4 button. I hit 5.

Step five: I walk down a flight of stairs, waiting long enough for the woman to find her office.

Step six: Hopeful of giving the impression that I come here often and am not looking at office numbers, I walk, casually down the corridor. I see 404 out of the corner of my eye and walk past.

Step seven: I stop in front of 408, look back quickly to see that the hall cleared and just as quickly step back to 404.

Step eight: I try the doorknob. It doesn't work. It's locked.

Step nine: For the first time, I notice a piece of yellow legal pad Scotchtaped to the door. "Gone to lunch. Back at 1 p.m." is scrawled in ink.

Step 10: I'm twenty-five minutes early. People have to eat. I back away slowly, my mouth open. I look left and right. I head back to the elevator (no one could know where I was going, I reason).

Step 11: I exit the lobby and head back to the car.

Step 12: I drive away, thinking of some way I can kill twenty-five minutes.

✦ ✦ ✦

When I say God has a plan, a time for each of us, I have reason to believe this. If something hadn't helped me at that moment, I wouldn't be writing this. I was terrified of going through that routine again. I was ashamed. I was embarrassed.

And so far I hadn't said a word to any human who wasn't related to me. The seriousness of this began to sink in, fighting past the denial. This might not be a problem that could be fixed today. Somewhere in the back of my mind, I had thought that I would go in to the service, get a pill or something, come out smiling, go home, maybe kiss and hug Mary, and watch the sky become a gentle red in the evening. Things would be good. I would have done it. Told it all. Confessed the problem. Got help.

Billy is special. Billy is good.

But that locked door shook me to the bottom of my shoes.

It gave me more time to think. I worried. I sweated through the car's air-conditioned coolness as I drove. Finally, fear welling in me like stomach acid, I parked in a shopping center lot, waited impatiently for a little man to finish using the phone, and did what I always did when I felt alone or useless or depressed (at least during the day; I never drank during the day). I called Mary.

Tearfully, I told her about what had happened. It seemed such a big problem. I couldn't cope.

Mary, God bless her, loves me. Loves me deeply. This I do know. But she told me the exact thing I wanted to hear but didn't need to hear at all. It could well have cost me my life. In an attempt to help the drunk, the codependent often does the opposite of what should be done. That is how the disease affects the loved ones in the house.

She said, "Baby, why don't you come on home and forget this. Maybe you can just slow down, just drink on the weekends. We'll get through this."

Oh, the joy. Pressure release valve. The green bean had an outlet.

God wouldn't let me. I believe that with total assurance now. It was nothing I did, nothing I decided. I was totally incapable of doing the right thing at this point. All I had to do was get back in the green Escort sport model I couldn't afford, crank the car and the tape deck, pop the moon roof and go home.

Delightfully. Cured of the mediocrity that was growing in me like so much cancer.

After all, I'd tried. If the door being locked wasn't an omen, what could it be?

But God wouldn't let me.

Something brought up an image of my walking into Mom and Dad's bedroom in the last week of his life and seeing Mom and my cousin wiping his own feces off his genitalia and slipping a Depends back on him. Drool was sliding down the side of an unresponsive chin; his eyes were fixed on the ceiling of the room he'd shared with Mom for thirty years.

In the space of mere minutes, I was presented with images of my children and my wife, of the guilt at having destroyed a previous marriage and of my son growing up without me, of lying to my boss when a reference on my resume turned up the question of my drinking.

Standing on the sidewalk of the Crescent City shopping center, sweat beading on my forehead, I made the first adult decision I'd made in a long time, maybe since I took that first serious sip of Budweiser back in Lizelia twenty-six years earlier. Setting my chin, I got back in the car and cranked it, heading to whatever passed for my destiny.

If I had known what I know now, the most sincere prayer of gratitude would have been in order.

✦ ✦ ✦

The session with the service worker went quickly. She merely asked me a few questions, mainly about why I thought I was an alcoholic. Amazingly, I didn't have much of a problem talking with her. I felt some shame, but I thought this was going to help. Or at least give the appearance of helping. So I offered answers the best I could. I told her about Dad. His drinking. His distance. I told her how much I had been drinking. Why I thought I couldn't quit. Why I thought I drank.

She was nice, offering smiles and assurance that I was doing the right thing. The meeting ended with her setting an appointment for me the following Monday at a local hospital. I really hadn't considered that I would be going to a hospital. I had thought that whatever would be done with me or to me would be done here, as though it were a psychiatry office.

The seriousness of the situation began to sink in as she explained what was to be a multi-week program. I would be in treatment for three weeks, then have meetings that could last up to ninety days. Ninety meetings in ninety days, she said.

That terrified me.

I had figured this wouldn't have to be known at work. My boss, a good friend, wouldn't have to find out, I had reasoned. That picture was being replaced by worries about what he and others would think of me. I felt so weak. I couldn't tell them all the stories, all the facts. I just couldn't. And without those facts, they couldn't see the real me but only the drunk who couldn't keep his life in order. I was full of shame at this point. While the young woman kept talking, describing the program, in my mind I was painting the future in black.

What had seemed so promising now seemed terrible.

I asked whom I should tell. She suggested the personnel manager and my boss, who after all, would need to know for scheduling purposes. The personnel manager needed to know on a quiet basis as part of the program. Since I was a self-referral, the upper management need not know.

I hadn't considered any of this.

I thanked the woman for her help, and walked away in a daze. This just hadn't gone the way I had thought it would. What had I gotten myself into? I decided on the drive back that if any of this was really to work, I needed insurance money. So I drove by work and went in.

I met first with the personnel director. I asked about time off, my vacation and sick leave situations. I asked how much my insurance would pay for. I talked a little about the problem. She was—a running theme—kind. She said she wanted what was best for me, and I believed her. She said the problem was much more common at our business than I would imagine. She also said she understood.

I then went upstairs, and, in perhaps the most difficult moment of the entire year, I asked my boss and two assistants to come outside.

Under the now-hazy New Orleans skies, in the shade of one of the many old oaks that ring our building, I tried to explain what was going to happen. Again, I lied a little. I told them the constant criticism from upper management, coupled with the complete lack of praise, had worn me down. That I drank over that.

That was true, but I couldn't tell them the full extent of the problem; I didn't even understand it myself at that point.

They expressed shock, but also thank God, support. They told me to do whatever it took to get better.

Had they done anything else, quite frankly, I wouldn't be writing this. Again, God speaks to us in so many ways. And though I don't know the depths of their beliefs, I now know the depths of their friendship. They were hugely important to my recovery. I drove home to an anxious Mary.

I believe we were beginning to understand that our lives were going to change although neither of us knew how much.

✦ ✦ ✦

That Saturday night I had my last drink. My last bottle. I talked Mary into it the way I had always done. "This is the last time, baby." Let me do what I love so much one more time. That was the rationale. But Mary talked me into at least drinking rum. When I drank whiskey strange things happened to me.

Ironically, it was on a trip to New Orleans in 1975 that I first drank Canadian Club whiskey. And the part of me that is an alcoholic had come home. It was Nirvana in a bottle. I could make a couple of stiff drinks (by the time Mary and I married, "stiff drinks" meant half of a half-pint at a drink) and feel the world come under my control. I thought I could talk and think more clearly, walk more upright, communicate ideas more easily. I could be the person I wanted to be.

Early in our marriage, Mary took away the whiskey. After finding me passed out in the bathroom or on the living room floor a couple of times, she was able to convince me that this was no way to live. On occasion, she relented. I never forced the issue. If I drank enough beer, I could get the same sort of feeling that whiskey gave me.

I didn't want another divorce. I loved Mary with all my heart. She loved me, too, and put up with more than a person should have to put up with. I wasn't a terrible person; I was lonely inside, sometimes depressed. I didn't drink all that much early in our marriage. When I met Mary, I was drinking a fifth of whiskey a night and just about out of my mind with loneliness. But she cured that, partly filled that hole, and the amount of whiskey I was drinking shrank.

But with an alcoholic, it never goes away. By itself, at least. I could go two or three days without something, and I would get fidgety. And there would be more beer. A weekend couldn't pass without my having something to drink on either Friday or Saturday.

After Shanna began playing softball at the age of eight, I would have beer following each game. It was the way to wind down. And the work on Saturday nights during football season, which involved putting together the biggest sports section of the week at the newspaper, was always followed by a quick six-pack. It took away the tremendous amount of stress. It was all that worked.

That last Saturday night was like many others had been. Mary in the living room watching something on TV, me in the bedroom watching a baseball game and knocking back rum and Coke. It was a pleasant drunk. I didn't pass out. I didn't head back to the store for more, as I had often done. (Mary had gotten me to start riding a bike when I went up to a convenience store to get more booze, so there wouldn't be the chance of getting hurt or hurting someone else. It made me feel like a little kid, but I agreed it was a sensible thing to do, at least until the time I had a bike accident and popped a couple of cans of beer on the ground.)

One thing that made me different from some of the other alcoholics was that I never drank in bars. I couldn't afford what I was drinking at home, much less in a bar. And I couldn't drive when I drank; Mary had helped me figure that out. I had been in a bar just twice since we moved to New Orleans four years earlier and only in a couple of others during the time we had been married.

But that contributed to the isolation I felt. Alcoholics become so alone and depressed. I drank in my bedroom, almost exclusively. The kids couldn't see Dad getting drunk, I figured. And no one else could, either. But that meant no one ever came over. Only once had someone I worked with been in my house. I was alone in this city, except for my family, or when I was at work. That thought never left me—except when I drank, of course.

Sunday passed without incident. I rested. We went to buy a few things, in case I was to be confined during the treatment. We didn't really know what to expect, but I had been told that there was a strong chance I would be confined.

When we arose on Monday, it was dark and wet. A steady drizzle was falling outside. Appropriate, I thought. I was filled with fear, but also, strangely, with anticipation. I had told everyone who needed to know, but I worried about what the others at work, who didn't know what I was doing but would surely notice my absence, would think.

Mary and I cleaned house, went over the bills that had to be paid, called the kids at my mom's. Around 2 p.m., we went to the hospital, to the addictive care unit. I was embarrassed even about getting off on the floor.

I met with a doctor who, to my surprise told me I would be going right over to the part of the hospital where addicts were cared for overnight or on a weekly basis. I would be held there for a week.

I was terrified. I was nearly in tears when I went out of his office, down the hall to where Mary was waiting. I told her what was happening. I asked her to walk with me across the hospital grounds, to pack a bag for me and to bring a pen and notebook when she came back later.

At 4:30 p.m., July 30, 1995, I checked in on the sixth floor of a treatment center.

At 7:30 p.m., I began a journal.

CHAPTER 3

Journal 1
July 30-31

Day 1, July 30

Dear Kids:

Is this the beginning of my salvation or the beginning of my insanity? Being a man of no discipline whatsoever, I do not know. I put myself in this position quite on purpose. I love to drink, but I know it is wrong.

And deep in my being, I also know I can't stop by myself. So here I am. I figure you force, pull, push whatever it is inside you that makes you feel you can possibly end your career by admitting you have a drinking problem to the people at work who need to know. You set the wheel rolling and you need no one saying, "Wait, you'll get better." I know I won't. So, forgive me for what I've done. I'm trying.

I met with Dr. John Glover for about an hour before he put me in here. Mary was in the lobby of the psychiatry waiting room, probably trying to hide behind a magazine. The routine was the second time I had been asked to explain my life with alcohol. Beer, with the occasional screwdriver, then Jack Daniel's on occasion, then Canadian Club, END OF FIRST MARRIAGE, Bloody Marys in Reno, back to Canadian Club,

SECOND MARRIAGE, weaned to beer, then here . . . after I answered yes to eight of the nine questions that determine if you're an alcoholic—when three would take you to the alcoholic Grand Canyon and stick out like a Reebok Shaqille O'Neal-sized for you to trip over—the decision was quickly made that I needed to be in detox.

I was admitted in a light-green T-shirt, new Reebok tennis shoes, and a pair of too tight jeans. They weighed me (218 pounds) and took my blood pressure (180/110) which seemed to alarm them greatly and that alarmed me greatly. They had me spell "WORLD" frontward and backward, which I believe I failed at, count backward from one hundred by sevens, fives or sixes (which I don't think I could do if I had never had a sip of alcohol), and remember and recite three words: "red tree house."

I'm also pretty sure that somewhere in there they tried to persuade me to embrace the use of the designated hitter. But it could have been the drugs.

Oh yeah, the drugs. Twice now I've been given something called Adaman or something like that. They explained that it takes the place of the beer, minus the beer gut, I imagine. Hey, I'm looking at something pretty good on the surface, but I know you can't grab a handful like so many sunflower seeds and watch a Braves game.

Detox, you must understand, is a prison. Humiliating, plainly and simply. They took my belt (no loss) and made me give it and my wallet to Mary, while keeping a maximum of five bucks. They took my cigarettes and lighter (major loss), and they won't let me have any sharp objects. It scares me to think about any of this.

But we'll see what Tuesday brings. I feel calm inside with a small headache and a bit of a queasy stomach. But I'm not seeing little butterflies on the wall or anything like that.

Oh, by the way, a hurricane is coming.

The things I get myself into.

Day 2, July 31

Whatever little euphoria I might have had is gone. I feel like Cool Hand Luke. I have to ask for my cigarettes and wait for someone to walk with me to a designated area where I have one or two while I am watched by a nurse. I don't know what would happen if I went over the fence, since I'm paying for this (albeit on a monthly basis probably). Mary is darn near strip-searched on her visits.

Today was the first day of school, though like much of college I spent the first couple of classes stoned. I swear I don't remember getting coffee from anywhere, but I had a cup in my hand. Today was devoted to—in my mind—pointing out the obvious. I have a disease. If the disease goes untreated, I go to watch Babe Ruth hit pitches. You know, he finished his career with the Boston Braves. Luckily, my liver turns out to be a heck of an organ. One worry down.

What to do with some of the classes, however. We had one teacher with a soft, demure voice. Seems she was responsible for teaching us to relax. She's greaaaaat at it. One little black man who said he could beat his crack habit by himself but was just doing this to please his wife had to get up from the soft circular sofa and sit in a hard chair in the back of the room. Me? I didn't stand on ceremony, or on anything else. I slid out of my chair onto the floor. I led the class in a chorus of no's when we were asked if we wanted to go for a long walk. The only long walk I was interested in was one that included a place to smoke.

After dinner in a little room with a view of the Mississippi River, I walked down to the social room. There were games, newspapers, books, a piano, and a TV. No smoking, but there was coffee. I had been taken off the drugs, and I was more alert. I didn't feel nervous or anything, but I was depressed.

There was an old man sitting in the room. He was the only person I had seen on the hall. Everyone else in class was on day treatment, meaning they were free to go home at night. The old man looked terrible. He was missing teeth, had sleep-flattened hair sticking up in spots, and was wearing an old, old terry-cloth robe.

I asked him how he was, and he said, "Fine. Well, I guess if I was fine I wouldn't be here, now would I?" He burst out laughing, which caused a fit of coughing. I shrugged, scared, really. I was in a psychiatry ward, after all. For all I knew, this guy was nuts. Imagine me, a fine upstanding deputy sports editor in with the nuts of society.

He finally walked away without a word.

I got up, switched the TV to WTBS and finished the evening by watching the Braves lose.

Ain't life grand?

CHAPTER 4

Treatment for a Lifetime

Who can straighten what he has made crooked?
When times are good, be happy;
but when times are bad, consider:
God has made the one
as well as the other.
Therefore, a man cannot discover anything
about his future.
—Ecclesiastes 7: 13-14

The doctors decided I was ready to be let out of the center after the second day. The hurricane alert might have contributed to that decision. I'll never know.

But for a couple of days, I was free. I was also scared silly. I came back on Friday for classes.

The classes had more to do with my inner self than with alcohol. They were designed to show me what had led to my use of alcohol as a crutch and to lift me by increasing my self-awareness and self-esteem.

They began at 8 a.m. and continued throughout the day, ending at 5. This particular Friday was my first complete day, the first day that I had to arise early, drive across the big bridge, and park at the center. It was my first day to walk into the building knowing I had a problem that separated me from the other patients, from the doctors and nurses who were going into work.

But it went okay. At first I found it difficult to get up that early, but it began to be my routine. I enjoyed the quiet in the morning, enjoyed having coffee out on the pool deck, the steam rising into the opening glow of the day. I liked reading and journaling in the morning. There was a peace then that I was beginning to dip into. The terror was starting to pass, as was the feeling of guilt. I had so much to be sorry for, but I felt I was finally doing something about it.

The morning, I found, is a special time for reflection. You can look at where you've been and try to get a handle on where you're going, which is, I believe, essential in stepping out of the world and into yourself. And that's a key ingredient in this journey. Not that you have the power of change, but if you never look at the parts of yourself that need changing and never look for help, the future isn't a bright one.

The members of my group came from all areas of the city, all walks of life. We packed into a very cold, very bright classroom. We sat in stiff-backed chairs, some taking notes, some watching glassy-eyed.

Alan was a white male in his mid twenties. He had a problem with marijuana. Although the addictiveness of that drug isn't severe, Alan couldn't stop using. He had a bad marriage—he'd separated a week before entering treatment—and a baby boy he missed terribly. His entire family drank to excess. His chances weren't good. His brother smoked marijuana without remorse and couldn't even understand why Alan was doing this. So there was no haven waiting for him when this treatment was completed. You soon learn that it is a good thing to change your environment, change your friends. Alan couldn't even hope to do that. He could divorce his wife if the pain and stress became too much for that fragile relationship. But he said that he couldn't leave his family. He simply couldn't.

Jerry was a short black man in his forties with a crack

cocaine habit. He'd never tried to quit, wouldn't have tried, but he'd been caught at work. They gave him a chance for treatment. He really didn't like the program but had no choice.

Jack was a black man in his late forties. After a week, I discovered that Jack was Jerry's supervisor. They'd even shared crack at times. Jack had been drinking and smoking crack for years. But the suicide of his son a year earlier had pushed him over the edge. He made good money, had a new marriage, said that overall he was happy. But this was his second try at treatment, and he didn't believe he had another try in him. His fear was death, not loss of job or even of his marriage. Drugs had ruined his life. He had worked his way into a good-paying job, into management even, but all was about to come crashing down because he couldn't cope with his life outside of work.

Bobby was an arrogant white man in his thirties. A business owner, he had spent most if not all of the profits on a cocaine habit. His wife had discovered how much money went up Bobby's nose and had thrown him out of the house. Bobby's future with his kids was in jeopardy and he'd turned himself in. His whole future was in question, he said, because he'd borrowed deeply from some guys who had a way of demanding payment. This treatment had to work for him so he could get the businesses back in order and pay his bills. He missed his kids, even his wife at times, he said.

Bobby would "graduate" during my stay. Others would come in. There was no starting point. You arrived, went right into the classes, and were joined with the others in the pain, apprehension and fear of the moment.

We bonded, despite our different backgrounds, in the way survivors on a life raft would bond. It was hold together or drown.

✦ ✦ ✦

Even though I had had no idea what to expect from treatment, I was still surprised.

We were taught time management, how to make effective use of your time by; 1) listing your goals and setting priorities; 2) making a daily to-do list, setting priorities from A-Z; 3) always starting your day with the A list, not the C list; 4) deciding what the best use of your time is right now; and 5) doing the top priority item right now. I sat there, writing everything down. That was just another game to win, it became obvious to me. So I made it my immediate goal to be the best in class. I had no idea, really, what this had to do with not drinking a beer, but these people had white coats on. That put them in front of the class while I sat in a hard chair.

We learned about crisis situations. When one occurs; 1) take a thinking break; 2) write down your options; 3) turn a crisis into an opportunity; 4) practice prevention of interruptions; 5) remove yourself from the crisis if you can't manage it; and 6) keep an interruption log.

We learned about self-esteem. 1) We must have confidence in our ability to make changes and realize we're important; 2) we must get control of our self-talk, thinking positive things; 3) we must take a daily inventory, writing good things that are going on with our lives; 4) we must have self-inventory—taking good care of ourselves; 5) we have a basic right to feel good about ourselves; 6) we must remember that arrogance isn't self-esteem.

We learned about relapse prevention, about good techniques for debating with the part of ourselves that rationalizes that it would be okay to have just a sip of beer. Just one can. Just one six-pack.

We learned about stress management, about methods of coping with anger, how anger turned inward is depression, about our unmet dependency needs from childhood, about assertiveness. We took communication training. We learned about discovering what the problem was in each situation and asking ourselves what we were doing to solve it.

We had a two-week crash course in feeling good about ourselves, about searching for the lost part of ourselves. And though one could argue that I am ungrateful, that the treatment obviously worked because I'm not drinking, I say that God used those doctors for one purpose: to turn me away from myself and toward a higher power. Through treatment, I found Alcoholics Anonymous. Through AA, I found God. And through the surrender to my Lord, I found help.

Nothing else works—no lecture on adaptational stress or on relationship dynamics or on styles of distorted thinking, although it was distorted thinking that had me feeling I wasn't a son of God. Nothing to do with false assumptions or the addiction process, about which I have pages and pages of notes, could have saved me.

These things did help me quit drinking, along with the fact that I spent so many hours in a classroom where they didn't sell beer.

I do not take away from their work. It does open you to ideas. But I thank God that the ideas that I began to open to were from Him. Everything else just made me want to work, to search, and to cry for more and more help.

Jesus told us that those who hunger and thirst for righteousness would be filled.

Three weeks of classes about life and how to live it only set me on course. They thought they were giving me a map I could take with me, but I was finding out almost as much about my life outside of those frigid classrooms, talking with everyone who came through the program about what had gone wrong with their lives.

The constant theme was a loss of God. A loss of being connected with God and with others. We, none of us, would ever be better, much less sober (and the two aren't exactly the same, for I did learn and do believe that alcohol or drugs are just the symptom of a greater need; they kill the pain momentarily, but they do nothing about the problem). That's the cruelty of the disease. Until we got out of our selfishness and into loving others.

And not ourselves. I disagree that I had to learn to love myself before I could love others. If that had been the case, I'd still be wandering like a lost sheep. I learned to forgive myself by understanding that God forgives me. I learned to forgive others by understanding that God forgives me. I learned to love because God loves me. I let God love me, and I don't worry about what I, or any other human, think about me. Well, most of the time.

✦ ✦ ✦

Three times a week they would pack us into an old, faded blue van to go to AA meetings across the city. At first one we went to, the shame and the fear returned. I'd been in treatment for almost a week, with time off for hurricane behavior. The meeting was held in a Salvation Army office room.

There was hot coffee, a stale donut. All of us there, from backgrounds as different as they could be, were bound together by what joined us. None of us could drink without sometimes horrifying consequences. There were DUIs beyond count. There were unpaid bills, lost marriages, lost children, lost opportunities, lost lives. There were young men and women whose love of the vine had kept them from completing college (as I suspect was the case with me). There were old men and women whose drinking habits had cost them all but the very breath that they drew.

What had been freely given by God, we'd wasted. Every one of us. None had come close to God, as Paul wrote.

It wasn't that we'd sinned by drinking. It was that by drinking we'd lost all contact with God. We'd dived into what the world had to offer in an effort to abate the pain of our failed lives, and all we'd managed to come up with as a solution was the death of our souls.

Every one of us.

Bill Wilson, one of the cofounders of AA, knew them all. As one of the few members who had dropped his anonymity, as one of the cofounders of the program and as a man of great honesty and courage and virtue, Wilson wrote what we all felt: "Could these large numbers of erstwhile erratic alcoholics successfully meet and work together? He wrote a book titled *Twelve Steps and Twelve Traditions of AA*, which I believe was inspired by God. I will talk more about that later. But now I will go back a bit.

✦ ✦ ✦

At the time of my divorce, I tried AA. I was drinking very heavily. It was nothing to drink a fifth and a half of Canadian Club. I was hurting more than I believed a person could hurt. I had not heard the idea that God never puts more on a person than he can handle.

Did I ever consider suicide?

I don't remember doing so. I am a coward at heart. Perhaps that saved me; my values did not, for the alcohol had drowned them. My religion certainly didn't, for as soon as I was a "man" I ran with the freedom that I thought that brought, away from Mama's God, away from Mama's judgment.

But AA didn't save me, either, at the time. I vaguely remember a few meetings, a few cigarettes smoked, a few sips of coffee in Styrofoam cups. I remember looking at the twelve steps, seeing God's name mentioned and pondering the implications. I wasn't about to start going to church, I could tell them that. One month dry and I began slipping shots of Schnapps. Then vodka, so my roommate wouldn't notice the smell. Then, what the heck, back to whiskey.

Twelve years later, here I was again, in an AA meeting. When I entered treatment, I never thought I would be back in AA. The prospect of attending meetings was alarming. If that was part of the "cure" and it hadn't worked before, even as I tried to salvage a marriage irreparably harmed and to get my son back, how could it possibly work now?

Was I truly doomed?

At least I tried. I committed to nothing more than the effort. Besides, they made me get into that van. Daily. Like condemned prisoners, we marched to dinner together, then smoked outside on the hospital grounds, then got into that ugly van with the air conditioner that grinned but blew little cold air.

To a meeting somewhere. Somewhere in a city that sells as much alcohol as any in the country.

We were the leftovers. The flotsam in the gutters. We were joined together without wanting it.

In a sky-blue van with a dark blue stripe, we journeyed to our salvation on potholed streets.

✦ ✦ ✦

After a few meetings, I began to open up, began to tell my story. And I found that I was able to be more honest about me and my condition, for I was among people who understood me, or understood that part of me that was so much like them.

I began to feel better about my chances, to get that old feeling of leadership again. So, I was an alcoholic. I couldn't help it. They told me I had a disease, and I bought that with all the credit cards I owned.

"Nothing I could do about it" was my sudden reasoning. I have a disease. What could I do?

The people at the meetings had the same disease, I was assured. Like lepers on the outskirts of the city, we clumped into the meetings, our skin intact but our livers asking for attention.

At one meeting, a man was filled with a gentleness and a glory that amazed me. He leaped around, smiling like a kid at Christmas, telling us his story and asking us ours. I was immediately taken with his enthusiasm, his joy.

That was what I thought I wanted. That's what this whole journey was about, I thought. I wanted his joy. If I could have, I would have robbed him right on the spot. Taken his joy home, distributed it like the candy I always bought the kids while I was buying Budweiser—to temper their feelings, of course—and gotten on with life.

That mansion veranda was calling me that night.

Then the counselor who had driven us to the meeting told me something I didn't understand at all.

"That's not what you want, Billy," he said. "He shouldn't even be doing that. He's only three months sober. He shouldn't be offering that much enthusiasm, that much happiness. This is a long road. It isn't easy, and there will be highs and lows that you can't possibly see a week and a half into your recovery."

I was absolutely crushed. I slept little that night. I refused to talk the next day. It was two days before anyone got anything out of me. If happiness wasn't the object of all this, what the heck were we doing there?

As Carolyn Arends wrote in *Reaching*, "We are reaching for the future, we are reaching for the past; and no matter what we have we reach for more. We are desperate to discover what is just beyond our reach. Maybe that's what heaven is for."

That's what I failed to see, to understand.

I knew nothing, but thought my intelligence would save me. I figured that after a week or two of meetings, I would be running the joint. I just needed to know what everyone around me knew, and things would be great.

I wasn't happy because I didn't know enough. I was sure of it. No amount of teaching that happiness wasn't what I was looking so darn hard for was going to make me believe otherwise. So I sulked. I didn't participate. I was so full of myself that I didn't contribute what I could have to the discussions. I pulled back, shut the old door that always had separated me from others.

They'd see. Yes, sir. They'd be the ones to lose.

And then a funny thing happened in a garage.

✦ ✦ ✦

Each class lasted for an hour. After the second one of the morning, we'd run outside or into the parking garage to smoke a cigarette or two. Misfits behaving accordingly.

Usually there would be the same number of people in the garage or outside the building as were in the classes. I find it amazing how many alcoholics smoke. The one seems to go with the other like peanut butter and jelly. Rarely do you see a non-smoking alcoholic.

But this time I am alone. There is no conversation, as there would normally be. (The conversations about the classes are where really I learn the most about myself and the others.) This time, however, all I hear is the roaring of the cars as they circle the up ramp and head on to the next floor to search for an open spot.

I light a Kool and inhale deeply, drinking in the satisfaction and calmness that nicotine and tar gives a smoker (along with a plentiful amount of carcinogens). I blow out a cloud, breathe in again. Calm myself with pollutants.

And the oddest sensation comes over me.

Something tells me this program will work if I allow it to. No question. No problem. Something calms me in a way nothing of this earth could. As the cars pass, I know a peace that surpasses anything I've ever felt. And my mind drifts.

It's 1961 and I'm eight years old, at a campground revival in Cuba, Alabama, a very small town on the west boundary of the state. The sawdust floor is a perfect playpen for shoeless feet. I slip off my shoes as the Church of God preacher begins to bray at us about hell, or some other subject that usually scares me into absolute submission, as much as a little eight-year-old can be. I am pushing my feet into the sawdust, feeling the stuff crawl between my feet. It is summer and the heat from the previous night remains, an unwanted visitor. I see thin cardboard handheld fans, with "Hardin's Furniture" written across the front and stapled to thin wooden holders, beating at the air like the baton of a conductor. Swish. Swish.

They might even help the air circulate. But I see sweat stains under armpits.

I feel the heat, the humidity. Sometime later, at the end of the sermon, as they have an altar call, I feel myself being called. The next thing I know, I am walking up the aisle between the two sets of folding aluminum chairs to the makeshift altar.

I begin to cry. I cry for all the sins I have committed. I cry because the people around me are crying. I cry because I am asking Jesus to be my savior, just like Mama and my aunt Bernece the missionary have always talked about.

I ask, and I believe I receive.

Now, in the garage, I look back over the years, through the mist of time that obscures objectivity and maybe even fact. I believe, and I understand, what were unclear moments earlier: that beginning then, in my childhood, Jesus was my savior forever. And all the alcohol I poured down my throat later didn't diminish that one iota. I just didn't remember. I didn't act the part. I didn't go in search of his word. I did nothing.

I am filled, I now understand, with the Holy Spirit. That's the emotion I saw in the man behind the AA podium, I believe. It's not the emotion that is the bad thing to have. It's the feeling that you've been saved, and that understanding is enough to send your senses reeling, like sticking your head into a bag filled with black pepper and sucking in the spice.

But if you don't allow God to continue on the path He's begun, you get someone like me. Washed up. Washed out. I had been washed away from that moment when I was eight until I wound up in this dirty garage.

✦ ✦ ✦

God grants us all wisdom, the scriptures say. And I can honestly say that in a dirty garage that morning, with time ticking away until the next class, I began to understand all that was happening in my body, in my mind, in my emotions.

I had hit a bottom. That bottom led me to seek help. That help led me to seek God. And God never disappoints those who actively seek him.

As an eight-year-old, I sought nothing. The next morning, my aunt Juanita came to get me. I had a little league baseball game that afternoon. All that Aunt Bernece and I had talked about, all the changes in my life that we'd planned, were forgotten. The feeling that had washed over me like an incoming tide washed back out to sea.

But that morning in the garage, with carbon monoxide fumes everywhere, the Holy Spirit reentered my life. Even if I didn't understand it. God's plan for me, which I believe included all that had happened in the interim, began to make a bit more sense. I had to be broken. I had to fall, or I didn't need a savior. All that I had done to myself and to everyone who loved me, all that had been done to me by the ones who loved me, simply led me to that moment. It is the understanding and belief that there is a plan, and a master behind the plan that gives us the peace I eventually sought.

The apostle Paul wrote, "Therefore, since we have been justified through faith, we have peace with God through our Lord Jesus Christ, through whom we have gained access by faith into his grace in which we now stand." (Romans 5: 1)

On reflection, I think I understood instinctively that this peace was being given, this grace was being offered and accepted. I didn't know at the time what was happening. I'd been talking to God for about a week, quite frankly because they told us to in AA, and I was trying to do what I was told. It was simpler that way.

But the answers I awaited, God speaking to me verbally, hadn't come. So I was going through the motions. I was absolutely stunned that morning to begin to get an inkling that there'd been answers all along.

I was back in the sawdust. And now I was being given an absolute second chance at life, not at a baptism, not at a church, but in a garage.

The rest of the day I was filled. As God filled me for the moment with his sweet mercy—just a taste, like one lick on the spoon after your mom has mixed the cake batter—I knew I had to have more. I knew this would work. I was given faith through grace. Before I asked Jesus for a second chance, which would come later in the journey, I was given faith. I knew—absolutely knew—I wouldn't fail.

I just no longer was trying. I was doing. Because for the moment the reins were taken from me. I wasn't in control, which was fine with me, for I knew I had done nothing with the control I thought I had. My best thinking, my best actions had gotten me into that garage.

I went back into class with a new perspective. I listened more intently, concentrated more, and contributed more. I had been given the faith to continue by a power far greater than I. There would be times when I tried to take the control back, almost always unintentionally, but I've never doubted who must be in control for me to succeed.

God was washing me clean. Who was I to question it?

I wanted more, and more, and more. So I began to hunger and thirst for knowledge of God. I wanted to be close. If it felt like this, I was for it. And although I've thought about drinking since I quit, I've never had the first urge to grab a drink. Not one.

The final week of treatment was a joy. I learned more and more about this disease and about AA. I found a temporary sponsor. I found a place where I could attend meetings on a permanent basis.

And when I left, with a bronze coin in my pocket that was given to each of the people who made it through treatment without stopping their cars at the corner bar on the way to the hospital or on the way home, I left with memories and the first real gratitude I'd known. It would open me up to the humility that is the key to acceptance of God's free gift of grace.

Without becoming broken, I wouldn't have admitted I was an alcoholic. Without that admission, I wouldn't have had the humility to admit I wasn't self-sufficient.

My problem with alcohol, which had at first been a way to

become part of the crowd, ended up separating me from people. That was humiliating. I had to reach this bottom, accept it and admit it, before I could listen to God. Truly listen.

I drove away from the hospital on that final evening, out of that garage, and as I crossed the Crescent City connection on my way home, I let out a shout of accomplishment. I had made it. I had done it. I no longer drank. My God, how had this happened? I had doubted everything.

I didn't have a clue, now, did I? I didn't understand fully. The credit was in the wrong place. I was a spiritually immature but seeking person when I left the hospital. I hadn't done anything.

CHAPTER 5

Journal 2
Aug. 18-Aug. 29

Day 20, Aug. 18 (meeting 15)

First day of freedom. I am scared to death. I slept a little later, until about 6 a.m., because I was just dead. I kept much of the same schedule though. My boss and I played golf and talked about everything. It went okay, I think. I still don't like working later in the evening, but I guess I'm dealing with it okay. I haven't drunk about it. Later, I went to work and was surprised that I didn't get the reaction I had expected. Almost none, in fact. I'm gratified about the way the family is trying. Mary is working on the house and her weight, doing what she can do, helping me any way she can. It is nice to see Shanna happy. And Carrie has lost her temper and her moods for now. But life is life. We have no money, the van is about dead, and my car started rattling badly.

Day 21, Aug. 19 (meeting 16)

Today was good, not great. I'm sober. So that's a start. We worked really hard on the house inside and out, and I just wore myself out. Carrie and I had a screaming match, so I guess life is life and all the sobriety in the world doesn't make things perfect. I'm working on my temper and my patience, but it doesn't happen overnight or even over three weeks.

Things weren't bad. My sponsor called, but I haven't really needed him—yet. Tomorrow, though, I want to start on my fourth step.

The question of the day is, do I go to a 6 p.m. meeting or an 8 p.m. meeting? I don't feel like a drink; I just feel bad. Things haven't gone all that well with the kids. I've lost my temper two or three times, even blew up at Mary. I don't know why. I'm really, really tired of all this new stuff. It's become a chore instead of fun. Here is where I've always quit.

I'm terrified I'll quit now. And I guess work is scaring me. I want to coach, and my new working hours may not allow it. I don't want to work nights; the meeting schedule is tougher that way. I want to see my kids, and my kids drive me nuts. Other than that, things couldn't be better. I still think about drinking. Really. Like it was something removed from me. I hate that I do, but I do. But I haven't felt that same old urge that I used to feel.

It's weird.

Day 24, Aug. 22 (meeting 19)

So-so day. Things went well early, then there was a gradual slide. Seems like I'm getting hold of sobriety and feeling good, and then it just darts away.

The old pressure comes back, and I forget that saying about "one day at a time."

It's hard to think about all these meetings and Mary and the kids being at home. And this stuff has to go on forever or I'll drink again. I cringe every time someone talks about slips.

Tonight I discovered we've screwed up on the checkbook, and it was scary and difficult to deal with. I was on the way to a meeting and I went ahead with it. So, in theory, I understand. It's just difficult to have so many meetings, to have to do so much to change or I fail. And they say that if I fail, I'll die.

I don't know why I feel any pressure.

Day 25, Aug. 23
I'm writing this on the morning of Aug. 24. Hit the wall last night. I lost my temper, ate two peanut butter sandwiches. Didn't walk and just generally felt like the weight of the world was on me. I went to sleep immediately. I have to understand that even with God's help, I'm human. And if I get too tired, I fail. No harm done. Just work harder to know the signs.

Day 26, Aug. 24 (meeting 21)
Again, again, again. I'm writing this a day late. And for sure a dollar short. It's day twenty-seven. I was worn out again last night, and, what's most frightening, I forgot to write. I also skipped out on the meeting after thirty minutes for the second straight night. I'm really worried that I'm going through the same old thing: start out being enthusiastic and gradually fall back until I quit whatever it is that I was doing. We walked extra, and I worked out on the exercise machine for twenty minutes.

Day 28, Aug. 26
I worked about four hours. I think I got too hot and too tired. And I went nuts. Screamed at Shanna. Then screamed at Carrie. Then went ballistic at J.C. Penney's, ironically over finding Shanna a dress so she could go to church with us.

Day 29, Aug. 28
Felt great today. Work went good. I got my thirty-day chip and was quite proud. No problems with my temper or any other character defects.

Day 31, Aug. 29
One month. Not a good day. At work I was short with some coworkers. My boss is getting on my nerves. I don't think he trusts me anymore. Why should he? I lied to him when he hired me. We need an insurance check that I've borrowed, or we might not be able to meet some bills we have. So, the pressure

is right square on me. But I know this too will pass. At least I don't yell at anyone anymore. It's becoming easier. No urges to drink. That's a positive.

CHAPTER 6

Peace of Mind

My heart is broken within me;
all my bones tremble.
I am like a drunken man,
like a man overcome by wine,
because of the Lord
and his holy words.
...Therefore their path will become slippery;
and they will be banished to darkness
and there they will fall,
I will bring disaster on them
in the year they are punished.
—Jeremiah 23: 9-12

One of the things I learned in treatment was that alcoholics stall in their maturity. When the switch is thrown that turns the drinker into the drunk, at that point maturity—spiritual and emotional—comes to a halt.

The train goes no farther down the track. You continue to make immature decisions. You continue to react on the emotional level, instead of on a mature intellectual level. The bills I accumulated were often the result of those kinds of decisions. I would get a credit card to pay off a credit card, for example.

I believe that point came with me with the first bitter swallow. I never grew. I never changed. I never found any spirituality. Everything was on the physical level; I never looked nor listened for God after the switch was thrown.

From that moment when I became an alcoholic, life was about me. What could I do? What could I buy? What could I own? What promotion could I gain? What did people feel about me? What could I do to make them like me? No joke was too outlandish, no bit of work too much, too hard, too this, too that.

As I drove out of the hospital parking garage, I weighed two hundred and five pounds. I'd lost thirteen pounds in twenty days, partly because I didn't like the cafeteria food, partly from the loss of calories that the beer had provided. I believe I was on the way to being a new person, outside and in. My blood pressure was now 110/70.

You can look for miracles everywhere, but as far as I'm concerned, I was becoming a walking, talking, complaining miracle. Gratitude had begun to blossom in me. But I was nowhere near where I needed to be.

I drove out of the garage and into life. And it scared the hell out of me.

✦ ✦ ✦

Thinking back to the beginning, the first three months of my journey, I can advise others: watch your emotions. I was a frayed electrical wire. There was a possibility of damage to myself, my family, my friends, the people who worked for me, the dogs, the cats, and ferret, the house, the shrubs. There were moments when I was more out of control than I had been before I found sobriety. Sometimes my emotions welled in me, and I snapped at someone or something, screaming like a madman.

The apostle Paul knew this feeling. He, like I, tried his best, tried to do the right thing. Wasn't that the point of this entire project—doing the right thing? Getting better? Getting well? But as hard as I tried, and I tried as hard, I believe, as a person could, I couldn't do the right thing most of the time. Paul wrote, "When I want to do good, evil is right there with me. For in my inner being, I delight in God's law; but I see another law at work in the members of my body, waging war against the law of the mind and making me a prisoner of the law of sin at work within my members. What a wretched man I am." (Romans 7: 21-25)

In short, I couldn't help it.

One day I would feel the rollercoaster start up the climb; I would reach the top and look at the cloudless sky and all that wonderful green earth stretching for miles. I would see the hope in the future and the delight in the present. And then that sucker would top the crest and head toward the bottom with me screaming all the way down. All I could do was hold on. Strap in for the long trip. Clinch the seat belt until my fingers were ghost white.

I bought a Bible, the Recovery Bible, and began to pore through it according to a daily plan written at the back of the book. I'd read AA's *The Big Book* and the *Twelve and Twelve* while still in recovery. I needed more, something deeper. I figured if I was going to talk to God each morning and each night, as AA instructed, I wanted to get closer to the source than Bill Wilson could make possible.

Depression became a traveling companion. I had thought treatment would be a way to get over the depression. But my nerves were so ragged, I would crash.

Ironically, I had more energy that I could remember ever having had before. I would wake up early, work out, do yard work, go to work, come home to more exercise, and finally slam into a wall.

Each movement was analyzed. Each misstep was regretted. I was trying so hard, hungering and thirsting with all my being, that I'm sure I rubbed many, many people the wrong way.

And I regretted even that.

I couldn't tell anyone what had happened to me. It's beyond irony. When we begin drinking, it's often to join that select crowd that is hip, to use an old expression. We want to belong. Eventually, for those of us with the problem, that separates us. I became isolated from others because of reasons I still don't understand. I couldn't hold my liquor so I acted the fool many times. That was all that was wrong, wasn't it?

Eventually the clown understands that this isn't funny any more. And the bragging about how much we can drink, or how we can drink and still function, stops. We don't talk about drinking at all. We're embarrassed.

When we stop, when we go for help, it's like a curse on us. A living millstone around our neck. We're shamed. We can't tell anyone that it feels like our toes are on fire sometimes. We can't tell anyone that while we have no urge to drink, shooting off a couple of strands of their hair with an air rifle is an appealing thought.

We just suffer through the emotions and go on, hoping against hope that we don't explode at the wrong person.

I prayed, knees hitting carpet regularly, to a God I didn't understand, though AA said I could choose. I knew only one God, the one I vaguely remembered from a sawdust covered floor. Somewhere deep inside I knew I couldn't go around making a mantelpiece or a fire hydrant my God, no matter what Bill Wilson had written.

I understand his intention. No one should be left out because of their beliefs. I understood that at the time, even thought it was a wonderful idea. No Jews should be eliminated from treatment, no Muslims, no Buddhists; none of us should be excised from the body alcoholic.

I don't think Jesus would want that, either. Our initial purpose was to stop drinking. I thought that would solve every problem.

If I had accomplished all that I had done at work while drunk, then sober, my family would have everything they wanted. And we would be happy. That veranda was calling on a daily basis.

The plastic coin they gave me to celebrate a month of sobriety cemented my thoughts. "All you have to do is have a goal," I thought. Look at this symbolism. I tried to quit drinking and I have. If I fail now, they'll still not be able to take this away from me. They told me the next period to celebrate would be at six months. I immediately set that as the goal.

I was praised by my boss for what I was doing. Praised by a grateful, prayerful mother. Praised by my wife.

I was accomplishing much.

And I was terrified I was failing. I couldn't pause long enough from all that I was doing to try to fill the large hole left when the drinking hours were eliminated. I couldn't see what was happening inside me, not from anything I was doing, but from being transformed by my Lord.

At the beginning of every AA meeting I attended, the group would recite the Serenity Prayer. Dutifully we bowed our heads and repeated, "God, grant me the serenity to accept the things I cannot change, courage to change the things I can, and the wisdom to know the difference."

Had I only been able to understand those words completely, to absorb their greatness, to understand the Father we were praying to, my fears would have vanished like the tears He will wash away one day.

But my journey hadn't been long enough.

Then three things happened that would point me in the right direction. I almost made it to the prescribed ninety meetings in ninety days, chose a home group as directed (the meeting I liked the most that I would call home base), and Mary and I took the kids to church.

And as part of the daily devotional, I read this piece by Gerald G. May:

Many people have burned out in ministries of service

> *and social action precisely because they have been worshiping their own activity instead of God. In such instances, burnout can be a blessed time that perhaps should not be forestalled. Burnout for the action addict is sometimes the only way he or she can come to know the difference between the means and the end, between good deeds and God.*
>
> *I do not look for God because I think it is what I am supposed to do. I do it because I need to, because of a longing that is not of my own creation. And though I often do try to substitute my actions for God because I can control my actions better than I can control love, I keep discovering that no good activity, no right attitude, no set of rules, no good feeling will ever satisfy my real longing for God. And now and then in especially graced moments, a flash of truly unconditional love bursts through me. Agape reigns for an instant.*
>
> *In that flash, my actions are determined neither by conscience nor by my desire. They come from pure, simple loving responsiveness to the needs of the situation at hand. They come from a love that is me but is not mine. I do not disappear in such moments, thank God. I am allowed to hang around and appreciate the beauty. I know it is a partial understanding, but sometimes I think the chief purpose of humankind is that there can be someone to say, "Wow."*
>
> —*The Awakened Heart: Living beyond Addiction*, Gerald May

There was no light that flashed. No burning bush. No immediate understanding. But that passage began to explain quite a bit.

The church that we selected was important to me because I had to work through some difficulties with the way I viewed religion. It was the first time I did something I believe was directed by God rather than a counselor or an AA member.

The eighty-sixth AA meetings were important because I never went to one when I didn't leave feeling refreshed, and because of the spiritual advice I received at many of them. Many were seeking God as much as I was. And many had answers I needed to know. Each person I met played a part in my continuing to take steps toward the ultimate goal: Jesus. I doubt many of them even knew this. But I believe God spoke through many of them.

You must learn, if you are to find the peace I've talked about, that this journey isn't a quick trip. It's like the following story.

✦ ✦ ✦

I have trained hard, worked for years to reach this moment. I lift weights, eat the right things, do all my coaches tell me. I am given the schedule for the event upon my arrival at the Olympic village. I take a little travel iron out of my bag and iron my uniform nicely.

When the day arrives, I am first at the track. I look at all the fans. My mother is there smiling and waving, as proud as she can be. My wife and kids are there, acknowledging both their sacrifices to my effort and their pride. My friends, and associates are there with little buttons on their shirts that read: "I know Billy."

Eventually the other runners come to the starting line. I kneel, getting my feet firmly into the starting blocks. None of the other runners do so. They don't even have starting blocks. Well, that is their problem. I have read what I am supposed to, analyzed the racing form and strategy, done everything better than any other athlete. I know this is the way.

The starting gun goes off, and I race away from the crowd, pumping majestically. I am fifty yards away from the next athlete when I hit the hundred-meter mark. I raise my arms, flash a smile, and look for the electric sign that would indicate a world's record. I slow to a halt on the sweat-covered track.

I turn to see the other athletes. They jog past the line and continue. My smile turns to a look of bewilderment. Where are they going?

I am baffled.

I breathlessly ask a race official what is going on, and he sadly tells me, "You are mistaken somehow. You trained for the hundred-meter dash and this race is a marathon."

I ponder my choices. I can race after the other competitors, but I know I don't have what it takes to run 26.2 miles. So I drop to the side of the track, bury my face in my arms, and sob so deeply that my chest hurts.

As I sit there, tears flowing like so much rainwater, a comforting hand touches my arm. I refuse to look up. I am a failure, again. I have done everything I could. Everything. Every little thing.

I cannot give more. I can't.

The hand persists, gently but firmly. It pulls me to a standing position. And the figure does something I would never expect. Instead of frowning at my defeat, he stoops to wipe away the grass that is sticking to my sweat-soaked legs. He sweeps away the dirt from my shoes. And he looks up into my face, lifts his large callused hands to my cheeks, and dabs at the tears.

He whispers, "Go on. If you run out of breath, I'll breathe for you. If you fall, I'll lift you back up. If you think you're going to fail, I'll succeed for you. If your side hurts so much you think you're going to die, well, I'll die for you."

He lifts his palms from me, but, still thinking only of myself, my journey, I do not notice the frayed round holes in those hands.

But I begin the journey again. Slowly. Again trying my best.

CHAPTER 7

Journal 3
August 31-September 29

Day 33, Aug. 31 (meeting 27)

Another day. Another weird step. Today I seemed to make my boss mad. Seems you can't say what you feel if he disagrees with that statement. Anyway, since that was one of the things I struggled most with, expressing my feelings, maybe that was a good step. When you're sober, all things are possible.

Last night on the phone after I talked to Jason, my first wife told me that she and Jason were proud of me. Somehow that made me angry, I think because I don't care whether she is proud of me at all. But I guess that's a resentment that someday I'll have to make amends for. Mary cleaned the house really well today in preparation for the bug sprayers coming tomorrow. We're down to forty dollars spending money and forty dollars of grocery money for the week. Not good, huh? I have the assertiveness pretty much down pat. Now to work on getting along with people. Maybe I went a bit too far.

Day 35, Sept. 2 (meeting 30)

The Lord will provide—two insurance checks arrived on the same day. Work was tough—twelve hours, hectic, stress-filled. But I stayed sober. I did sleep until 11 a.m., which is the first time past 7 a.m. since I started, and I don't have the burning desire to go to a meeting that I have had sometimes, and I ate a peanut butter sandwich about 1 a.m. But I haven't really broken. This too shall pass.

The thing to remember is that five weeks ago I was drunk on a fifth of rum. Since then, the house has been cleaned and sprayed for bugs, I've lost seventeen pounds, Mary has lost ten, work has improved, family life has improved. The bills are the bills, but Jesus said, "Do not worry about your life, what you will eat, what you will wear. Life is more than food and the body is more than clothes . . . who of you by worrying can add a single hour to his life? Since you cannot do this very little thing, why do you worry about the rest?" (Luke 22-23/25-26)

I can't fix the bills in a day or two, so I'm not going to worry about it. Period. God will provide me a way to do this, I pray, if it is His will.

Day 36, Sept. 3 (meeting 31)

This is an in-case writing. I'm working late tonight. It will be late. I will be tired. So in case. Saturday was great. Just great. No blow-ups. No tantrums. Spent too much money, but I'm learning. I didn't do any step four work, so I hope to try again tomorrow. Did get my guitar. It will be tough to learn to play, however.

Day 37, Sept. 4 (meeting 32)

Today was tough. I felt good, really good. And I thought about how good a beer would taste. And it aggravated me. Aggravated me that I couldn't have one despite being sober for over a month. Aggravated me that God hasn't cleansed these thoughts from me despite all I've tried. But I went to a meeting, went to work, got a tape for Carrie and watched it with her—*The Adventures of Yellow Dog*—and teared up at the end. And that too passed. God prevents if you let God. If you let go and let God have the problem. I now realize I spent way too much money this weekend. It was my version of a dry drunk. With God's help, that too will go away.

Day 38, Sept. 5

I hit twenty pounds of weight loss today, and so WHAT? I can't think of one single thing that made it better for me. We mailed a letter and a two-hundred dollar check to AMEX today, explaining our difficult situation and telling them we'll pay two-hundred dollars a month until it's paid off. We're starting (or I'm starting) to get responsible.

Day 39, Sept. 6

. . . I'm depressed. And the bills are piling up. I try not to worry, try to put it in God's hands. But it's hard. Very hard. I said, in jest, to Mary that maybe I would just declare bankruptcy and move back to Mama's. Mary suggested that I go by myself so the kids wouldn't have to leave all they have here. Not the best words to begin a morning, huh? . . . .

Day 40, Sept. 7

See, a great day shall come. All of a sudden, we're gonna hire some help for me at work. So I won't have to work at night and spend so much time in front of the computer. Praise God. I called Jason and asked if he could buy his own train ticket, and he had no problem with that at all. That was beyond embarrassing. I've worked twelve of the past thirteen days, often ten hours a day, and I survived. Sober.

Day 43, Sept. 10

Well, I can't say parenting is going that well. The kids don't want to go to church. Shanna says she's got one dress and she's worn it. Carrie, well, just doesn't want to get up. Reminds me of me.

Day 47, Sept. 14

I felt somewhat non-spiritual today and that's fearsome. All you can do is surf with the feeling and wait for God to let the good feeling return, but no alcohol. My weight has stayed about where it was as I approach seven weeks. A plateau is where I am, in my weight loss, my spirituality, my recovery. I want more. I want a deeper relationship with God, with life. I want change. I want something. On some level, I feel something is still missing. I can't go backward. I can't seem to find the way to go forward. There's no doubt my life is better.

I can't argue with that. But quite frankly, what worries me is that I see a lot of people who have some sobriety and they don't really seem to have it completely together either. I guess life is just life and this program and God don't give you all the answers for a perfect life.

There are no perfect people, but I just keep coming to it, trying to achieve it. No question that I'm better at work. But that's not why this began. I'm spending almost no time with my family. Where is the good in that? I understand it's only for a few months. And it's terribly important for me. But it's hard. If it was softball season would I so happily go to meetings or work late?

Day 48, Sept. 15 (meeting 43)

A very interesting day. Sometimes it is so fleeting. I kind of crashed at the meeting tonight. A lot of questions just bubbled up. My spirituality dried up. Whap. All of a sudden I was questioning why my higher power doesn't make it easier to have the relationship I want.

I mean, if I had a friend or a loved one who wouldn't respond to me when I called, would I keep or maintain the relationship? But I have to or I drink, and if I drink, I die. Quite a paradox.

I want to live, really live; I want a good life. I want a good house, happy kids, a good relationship with Mary. A nice everything. Maybe that's the root of the problem. But where is the solution? I guess I can fake it till I make it, like some of the guys say. I'll do everything, anything. If this doesn't work, it won't be because I didn't do everything I could. And I don't know where this has come from. It just popped up after a good day. But honesty is honesty. I have to be honest about any doubts or fears.

Day 52, Sept. 19

Absolutely the worst day I can remember. Depression set in and never left. Why? Bill collectors calling, lack of faith, Jason, Shanna, work. Me. I'm sick. Sick, sick, sick.

Day 53, Sept. 20

Good God. It came back. As quickly as it left. I'll probably never know why I felt so bad. But it left. I do know I can't ever play God or question God again. My boss said something true today, which I didn't know he had in him at all. You can't get anything spiritual when you're asking for it or looking for it. It's a gift from God, and it'll come when you least expect it. I don't have all the answers; I might not have any. But I do realize that until I shut up and listen to God, I'll never learn anything. Someone said that the dumber I get the more knowledge I gain. That's true, I believe. The more I get rid of the pride, the self, the more I learn from God and the fellowship. I just truly hope I don't have to reach that sort of bottom again to learn a lesson. It's painful.

Day 56, Sept. 23 (meeting 52)

My psychologist suggested I quit calling days good or bad and number them from 1 to 10. So, today was a 7. It's been a strange, wonderful week. Good, bad, good, bad. But I've learned from each day.

My psychologist suggests that my goal through all this should be peace, instead of happiness. He says I have an unrealistic idea of happiness that I've had nearly all my life. Seems like I envision happiness this way: I would never lose my temper, the kids would always be hugging each other and obviously loving themselves and each other. We would be in a big, clean house with a wraparound porch and a big, clean yard with lots of sweet-smelling roses. In the country.

I still have a picture of lying in bed, the big fan we'd bought at the Meridian library blowing in cool, clean air on my face, listening to Credence Clearwater late at night. John Fogerty debuting "Green River" on WLS-AM out of Chicago. Brand new, never heard. Maybe heard just by me.

That's happiness to me. Serenity. Bliss.

That part of me died with a bad marriage, bills, work, age, and especially alcohol.

Responsibility wiped away my serenity, because I couldn't manage my life. I relied on wives and Mama to do that. When I took over, things went bad. It took this long for God to let me receive this gift.

Day 57: a 6.

Day 58: an 8.

Day 59: a 4.

Day 60: a 7.

Day 61, Sept. 28
I think the theme of the week was tired. I don't think I lost any weight this week, and I've probably eaten more and exercised less. I lost my temper at work today. I apologized. A 6.

Day 62, Sept. 29
Two months. Have you ever drunk coffee on an early fall evening, watching a pink sun set behind magnificent trees surrounding a golf course? Just sat in the quiet and soaked it in like a dry field absorbs a steady rain?

I suggest it. It'll give you a 10.

CHAPTER 8

Stepping Out

1. We admitted we were powerless over alcohol that our lives had become unmanageable.
2. Came to believe that a power greater than ourselves could restore us to sanity.
3. Made a decision to turn our will and our lives over to the care of God as we understood Him.
4. Made a searching and fearless moral inventory of ourselves.
5. Admitted to God, to ourselves, and to another human being the exact nature of our wrongs.
6. Were entirely ready to have God remove all these defects of character.
7. Humbly asked Him to remove our shortcomings.
8. Made a list of all persons we had harmed and became willing to make amends to them all.
9. Made direct amends to such people whenever possible, except when to do so would injure them or others.
10. Continued to take personal inventory and, when we were wrong, promptly admitted it.
11. Sought through prayer and meditation to improve

our conscious contact with God as we understood Him, praying only for knowledge of His will for us and the power to carry it out.

12. Having had a spiritual awakening as the result of these steps, we tried to carry this message to alcoholics, and to practice these principles in all our affairs.

My life was such a rollercoaster of emotion, coldness, raw nerves, and temper tantrums in the first three months of recovery that I was probably even more difficult to live with than I had been before. I wasn't out of control, but for the first time I thought I had no control at all.

People everywhere were talking about doing God's will. And I didn't know what His will was regarding me.

So I did what I always did. I read. And tried to win the game. I researched the program I was in.

I figured I needed to know what I had gotten myself into if I was going to be able to make it work.

The following excerpts are from an article by Tim Stafford about the spiritual roots of the Twelve Steps of Alcoholics Anonymous.

> *Bill Wilson was unquestionably the most influential person in the development of Alcoholics Anonymous. In 1934, he was a grandiose, loud-talking New York City alcoholic. Nearly 40, he was feeding his habit by stealing grocery money from his wife's purse . . . .*
>
> *One November day, an old alcoholic friend, Ebby Thatcher, paid him a visit. Thatcher was sober and had come to tell Wilson why. He had had a religious experience. Members of an organization called the Oxford Group had visited him in jail, where he had been incarcerated for drunkenness, and he had yielded his life to*

God. The desire to drink was gone, he said.

> After several visits, Thatcher convinced Wilson—who was quite averse to religion—to attend a meting at a Manhattan rescue mission sponsored by Calvary Episcopal Church, local headquarters of the Oxford Group. Wilson, though quite drunk, was moved by the testimonies and went forward to testify to his own changed heart. This change lasted less than a day. Wilson went on a three-day binge and was hospitalized again.

Thatcher visited the hospital, and at Wilson's request, repeated his formula for conversion: "Realize you are licked, admit it, and get willing to turn your life over to the care of God." After Thatcher left, Wilson fell into a deep depression. But finally, while still in the hospital, he found himself crying out, "If there is a God, let him show himself? I am ready to do anything." What followed was a powerful spiritual experience in which Wilson felt overwhelmed by a sense of freedom, peace and the presence of God.

He never took another drink.

Wilson joined the Oxford Group and attended meetings at Calvary Church, pastored by the Episcopalian Sam Shoemaker. Early AA converts, who would eventually write the text that was given to me when I was in the middle of treatment, (I devoured it as if it were a fresh steak; it was my first step toward the path Christ walked), got their ideas of self-examination, acknowledgment of character defects, restitution for harm done, and working with others from the Oxford Group of which Thatcher had been a member. Wilson, who I believe to be a great writer and a great spiritualist, did not want to eliminate anyone from the opportunity to be saved from this deadly disease, so he didn't push the spiritual aspect of the program at first.

When he and others formed groups to write the steps of the

program (originally six steps), he said he was surprised at how often God was mentioned.

(To me, the twelve steps seem very much like the beatitudes. The ideals are the same.) The AA groups, by the way, eventually left their alliance with the Oxford Group because they thought the group was too religious, too willing to focus on Christ instead of the problem with alcohol.

At no point did anyone ever tell me I couldn't say Jesus Christ was my higher power. But there was an unspoken suggestion that we not impose our beliefs on others at the meetings. The fight against alcohol was the only fight to be conducted.

For the first three months, I was trying not to spit the bit. The God of Abraham, Isaac and Jacob was my higher power from day one. But surrender? That was a few steps down the road.

I was dancing as hard as I could, trying to understand what I was doing.

✦ ✦ ✦

I completed the first three steps of the twelve step program to the best of my understanding while in treatment.

My understanding included the facts: According to Hazelton Foundation's *Little Red Book*, published in 1957 as a supplement to AA's *Big Book*, alcoholism is a disease of one's physical, mental, and emotional states. A development of humility, honesty, faith, courage, gratitude, and service is essential to defeating the disease, which, if one slips away from the program, is advancing even while one does not drink.

I took those words to heart and tried to develop all those characteristics. And I was being defeated on a daily basis as my emotions ranged all over the board. I tried my best. I tried to absorb and accept the saying "one day at a time." But one day at a time I failed. And the guilt grew slowly, even as my efforts were building speed.

I read in *The Little Red Book* that spiritual bias is but self-will that does not yield to reason. "Trying to understand God's will for us is not hypocritical. It is a basic recovery principle for alcoholics. It never fails those who sincerely use it." So I tried. I prayed in the morning reciting what AA calls the fifth-step prayer, asking God only what his will for me that day was. And if I was getting an answer, I couldn't figure it out.

Luckily, the writers of *The Little Red Book* and of my *Recovery Devotional Bible* (which I recommend highly) knew some of what I was going through. They advised that a great barrier in finding God is impatience.

They also advised that we soon learn that spiritual attainment must be earned. I don't agree with that now, but I accepted it at the time. And tried all the harder.

But I slowed to a crawl, as everyone kept telling me to, when I reached step four. I couldn't understand what I was supposed to do. I wanted to do it perfectly. I didn't want to make a mistake.

I embraced the meetings because I could talk at them, I could smoke at them, and we talked about God a lot. All that appealed to me. This wasn't my mom's church, where what you wore or how you did your hair made you part of the in-crowd. I was one of these people. No one was worse or better than anyone else. We seldom even mentioned last names.

It was at one of these meetings that I took another step spiritually. I met Harry.

✦ ✦ ✦

"In those days John the Baptist came preaching in the desert of Judea and saying, 'Repent for the kingdom of heaven is near.' . . . John's clothes were made of camel's hair and he had a leather belt around his waist. His food was locusts and wild honey. People went out to him from Jerusalem and all Judea and the whole region of the Jordan. Confessing their sins, they were baptized by him in the Jordan River." (Matthew 3: 1-2/4-6) Harry's desert is a place called the Camel Club, so named because the beast can go a long time between drinks. It is where I decided I would go to meetings when I came out of treatment. It is closest to the house.

The club is an old cinder block building. It rents a room for AA and one for Al-Anon meetings. The meeting room is smoky, often dirty. But it is there that God really began to talk to me. Listening to story upon story that I could relate to, having a place where I could tell my worst secrets, where I could express my fears and disappointments when even Mary couldn't understand, turned out to be critical in my spiritual journey.

As was meeting Harry.

Harry doesn't go there often. Just drifts in when whatever drives him tells him to. He goes there to help. That's what Harry is all about—helping others, because Jesus had helped him.

Harry has a belly that would shame Santa. It is huge, and his belly button is an outie. I know this because he wears dirty shirts that are just a size too small and inevitably that belly button sticks out like a hitchhiker's best friend. His hair stands up in various places. In others, it is slicked down by who knows what. He is missing some teeth. He walks with a pitiful limp.

The first time I heard Harry talk, I couldn't understand him. He talked slowly, and sometimes in the middle of a conversation he would stop and look around as if his next words had run off to hide. Seconds would pass, and Harry would start over at the beginning. He loves to talk, through it all. He loves to talk about God. About what God can do for you. About how God is the only way you can beat this devil alcohol. He corners newcomers, first-timers, or simply people he doesn't remember, and he rattles at them until they can think of some way to break away. If they are kind. Some simply walk off as Harry is talking. He will continue for a couple of moments, then slowly drop his head and limp away.

He knows the twelve steps by heart, which is good, because he isn't able to read.

Harry corners me about two months into my journey. He

again tells me what I'd heard him share at meetings. He tells me about God. He tells me about how he feels now. He tells me what God will do for me if I will surrender my life to Him.

It takes him many minutes to get that out. And I try to drift away, backing slowly down the old hallway. Finally, I tell Harry I have to go to the rest room. He follows me in. And keeps witnessing for God.

Harry usually speaks at the end of the meeting, and usually the chairman tells him to keep it short. But once, at a sparsely attended meeting, Harry was the first to speak.

I'll never forget what he said.

Harry talked about his mother leaving him when he was a kid, about going to jail for the first time when he was nineteen, about eventually being sent to the penitentiary. He talks about being committed to several sanitariums, and about being given shock treatment (it ki-nd of af-*fects* the *way* I spe-ak). He talked about getting out of the second sanitarium, without a home, job, or a family (I h a da kid). He lived under a bridge near the Camel Club, eating garbage and stealing money (struggling down dark lonely streets with a limp and a bad eye from being hit with a baton in prison). And always, when he was not in prison or in a hospital in a straightjacket, there was booze.

Until he found Jesus.

I know some people think I changed for the worse. I know they don't understand my journey. But if I could take everyone reading this book to meet Harry and spend fifteen minutes with him, they would know. They would understand.

Not immediately maybe.But on some quiet night, when they were pondering why things weren't the way they wanted life, when the motor on the swimming pool timer had blown, or the car was rattling, or some bill just couldn't be paid because they had spent too much somewhere else, they could remember Harry. There but for the grace of God go I.

Paul wrote: "You see, when we were still powerless, Christ died for the ungodly."

While I was still unsurrendered, God led me (and many, many others) to Harry. And we learned.

✦ ✦ ✦

But that fourth step just wouldn't get done. Finally, a new sponsor told me to write a relationship list, describing my relations, then to write a list of all the people I had resentments against and why.

At first I balked. I didn't resent anyone, did I? Then I wrote page after page. And I began to understand.

First, however, was the relationship list. (May they forgive me for my honesty. Thank God we've all grown since this writing.)

Mary: I love her most. But until now, I resented how tired she gets, how little she did at home, how little she disciplined the kids, how she had little desire to help with the responsibilities. I wanted her to stop me from drinking, because I couldn't stop myself. I wanted her to make the bills be paid on time, to make the kids behave and to keep a house like Mama's. I wanted her to take charge. Because I was opting out of life. I loved her because she refused to do those things. I loved her because she is selfless. She reads. She tries to change even as I do. Neither of us is perfect. But through God, we're trying.

Shanna: She is a complex kid. I never really know what she's feeling or thinking. She doesn't seem to particularly care about us, or at least she seldom shows it. I can't come close to getting her to be the way I want her to be emotionally. I want her to be as happy and involved with her parents and her sister and brother as she is with her friends. And I wonder why she never has a friend to sleep over, but always goes to their houses. I believe she is smart and well liked. I believe she has some problem with Carrie. Maybe I've been roughest on her when I was drinking. Maybe that made the chasm that seems to exist.

Carrie: My most difficult problem. She drives me crazy

sometimes with her moods, her fears, her tantrums. I guess she is most like me. She's also the kid most likely to be helped by my sobriety, I believe. She can be funny and independent. And she can cling to us like any of those tree monkeys. She is scared of the dark and of spiders. She has a TV in her room, but doesn't like to be in there by herself.

But I hate it when Shanna stays in her room by herself. So I can't be happy. I had a thought that maybe I struggle with our kids so much because I wanted our family life to be like what I wanted my life with Dad and Mama to be. Unfortunately, I became Daddy, and I wanted my wives to become Mama. That caused friction in both marriages. And my kids test my patience level because they don't act like those on TV, which was the only place I saw what I thought were truly happy people.

Jason: I don't know him, really. He seems to be a good kid—almost too good. He sometimes says what he thinks you want him to. I haven't seen him angry or sad in years. Not seen what's inside him. I worry that the divorce and my drinking hurt him so much. And I wish beyond wishes that he had grown up with me, or I with him. But it just wasn't God's will, I guess. I hope Jason and I get closer to each other, but I've written him once in two and a half months of sobriety and he hasn't written. I hope and pray he knows I love him. Actions speak so much louder than words, don't they?

I also wrote on the relationship list about my mother, my friends, and about the people I work with. But I don't believe those have had such a great effect on my life.

And then there was Daddy.

CHAPTER 9

Journal 4
September 30-October 29

Day 63, September 30
A learning day. Seems I learn more from the bad experiences. I was up and down today. And the down was for no reason. I yelled, cursed, and threw a phone over the matter of Shanna's boyfriends calling. Those are things I just can't change. I must accept them. I can, however, cancel call-waiting. Should I desire to. But I don't need to take it to that length. Yet. A 7.

Day 64, Oct. 1
The best way to understand powerlessness is to experience it. That comes from my sponsor, Jimmy. The new improved sponsor. He's helping me with the steps. He told me to write down everything people called me. To go through the steps, work on them on a written basis, then live them. It takes time. It lets you take a thorough look at the list. A 6.

Day 65, Oct. 2
Another 4. I have a hard time understanding when I'm doing God's will and when I'm doing my own. I'm willing to get out of the way, but I'm not sure I know how to at times. And I'm worried about my behavior at work. I'm being very quick to lose my

temper. I have less patience, and I seem to be of less good humor. I almost never quit working. Maybe I'm just overly tired because of the stupid Macintosh computer. I just felt my wheels spinning in every direction today.

Day 68, Oct. 5 (meeting 63)

A 7. A funny sort of day. Things were nearly perfect. But I just felt something was missing. Don't have a clue what. It's hard to settle for peaceful. It comes and goes so very easily. But I'm looking forward to going to Mama's.

Day 69, Oct. 6 (Meridian meeting 64)

A 7. I had a nice, peaceful drive up here. Mama was very happy to see me, as was my cousin. I miss Mary and the kids, but this is something for Mama. Kind of giving back in the only way I can. I still feel we should talk about the past, but maybe that needs to wait until I make amends. I had the thought: Why would my kids want me to be around all the time when I really don't want to be around Mama all the time? I guess it's natural.

Day 70, Oct. 7 (meeting 65)

An 8. It couldn't have been much better. Great weather. Good drive home. I bought Mary the rug she wanted. Mary's check came. Bounced a check, but what the heck? I'm stupid. Perhaps the best thing was that, by trying a little, I didn't disappoint Mom. And by letting go of some of the things I felt about growing up—not telling her about it but feeling it—I felt better about the simple act of not hurting her.

Day 71, Oct. 8 (meeting 66, church)

A 3. It stank. I blew up at work. And just didn't care, really. My boss and I have some problems, of my own doing, that are going to have to be worked out. Shanna disregarded the time I had told her to be home. The peace and love and warmth I had felt this weekend were destroyed. But I hit 170 pounds. Incredible.

Day 76, Oct. 13 (meetings 71,72)

A 10. Honest. Things just couldn't have been much better. Let me count the ways and praise God: 1) We got a check for $142 from a lawsuit I wasn't even a party to for a car I sold three years ago. 2) We found one hundred dollars in the bank we didn't realize we had. 3) I'm sober seventy-six days, by the grace of God. 4) I understand more about God's will. 5) I had a good meeting with my psychologist. 6) The Braves lead the Reds 3-0 in the NLCS. 7) Shanna and I had a tiff, but then I thought it over and talked it over with her and we wound up going to the mall together. Her mood picked up immediately. 8) I had a great low-fat dinner, and I'm eating low-fat chocolate ice cream as I write this. 9) Carrie was great. I told her to pick up her shoes and she started to pout, but I turned it around by making her come to me. I took her shoes, threw them in the air, and made a face. She smiled—picked up her shoes and went on. 10) Mary is a great, wonderful, understanding, supportive wife. 11) I have my God. 12) Even if I can't play golf, I can learn from it. Play one shot, one hole at a time. Focus on the shot, not the outcome or the next shot. Take what happens and go on. It's the same with recovery. One hour, one day at a time. Enjoy the day. You might never have another 10. God only knows. And I thank Him for this one.

Day 79, Oct. 16 (meeting 75)

A 4. I seemed to be tossed and turned emotionally today. But the center is easier to find now in days like this than it was. I was a step or two from losing my temper a couple of times today. But I fought to maintain—easy does it. I hollered at Mary and even at God at one point over nothing, but I quickly asked both for forgiveness. Just a smidgen of worry creeps in every time I don't watch it. I bought *The Little Red Book* tonight, and I feel I did at least one thing for my sobriety today. I'm worried as the third month draws to a close. Peter wrote that perseverance gives us hope. Perseverance is the biggest hole in my life.

Day 82, Oct. *19 (meeting* 78*)*
A 5. Up and down. Up and down. I was tired at times, serene at times. When will this end?

Day 83, Oct. 20 *(meeting* 79, 80*)*
Well, I broke. A 3. Here's what happened: I was playing golf. I was using what my psychologist had told me. I began spraying the ball all over. So I decided this crap didn't work. If that didn't work, what else was there I'd been taught that didn't work? Before it was over, I questioned everything. And I finally quit the game, walked off the course. It gets so hard sometimes. I want to believe, I want to be good, I want to be better, I want to be, well, perfect. And I fail at everything. I just hate failing. I hate not being the best at a single thing in my life, or anyone's life. And if I fail at my sobriety, it's just another in a long line of failures. I'm mixed up. Confused. Depressed. Doubting my faith. Failing, again.

Day 84, Oct. *21 (meeting* 81*)*
Where does the insanity come from? Why can't you just read what you're supposed to do, do it, and find peace? If God is as loving as He must be, why is this as hard as it is? It would seem the thing would be to do as God says, like a child following his parents' wishes, and you would be rewarded. Yesterday, I wasn't—to my knowledge—trying to do my will as opposed to God's. I wasn't concerned about score or winning on the golf course. I was focusing, and things just fell apart. It's toughest to be spiritual when things are rough.

I pray I continue to work at this. I'll begin my step four a week from Tuesday. Halloween.

And go for a month. Writing about my life and what the events show me about my character flaws. Where does this need for perfectionism come from?

Day 85, Oct. 22 (meeting 82, church)
Church was good. We're talking about starting a Thursday Bible study group, which would be good. Work was hectic, stressful. I weighed in at 166.

Day 87, Oct. 24 (meetings 84, 85)
A 1. Absolutely the worst day since I've been sober. I got a 1 only because I didn't drink.

Day 88, Oct. 25 (no meeting, just couldn't make myself go)
I'm a nut case dressed up as a responsible adult. Slip a white shirt and a tie on a drunk, and you get me. None of this is easy. None. No matter what anyone says. To change your whole life, your whole way of thinking, couldn't be harder. It ain't just about not drinking. Quite frankly, that's been the easy part. It's about the way you think on an instinctive level. I don't like adversity. I run from it. So that's the reason I medicated problems. That's the reason for changing jobs. That's the reason for all those loans. A quick fix.

That's me.

If there is something about the Bible that troubles me, I quit.

Exercise? For a short time. Everything has to be quick. Well, it's been right at three months. I'm at the point where I must decide to go on or give up. And I'm frayed at the edges over it. It sure doesn't help that the World Series is going on at the same time. As crazy as it sounds, the Braves winning or losing the series is huge to me. Huge.

The Braves are up 3-1 in the series. I know, however, that they'll lose and kill me again. Neither I nor any team I ever follow wins the big one. It just doesn't happen.

Day 90, Oct. 26
Prayer in Numbers 6: 24-26—"The Lord bless you and keep you; the Lord make his face shine upon you and be gracious to you; the Lord turn his face toward you and give you peace."

Here I am. ninety days into recovery. My psychologist says only one third of all treated make it this far. And me? I'm wavering. Faltering. I let the world—in the form of the Braves—back into my life. I hurt, over some stupid baseball team. UGGGGHHHH. But I want to stop to be grateful. It helps to stop and think about the changes.

1) My weight. I've gone from 218 pounds to 168; 2) my endurance; 3) my work (never been better); 4) my relationships (I'm more assertive at work); 5) we haven't charged anything in three months; 6) we're paying off all the overdue stuff.

The list shows improvement. But the character defects remain, just as they were. There have truly been spurts of spiritual experiences, moments of patience and love, but the feelings of doubt, self-pity and all the other stuff are fighting their way into me again. The only solution, after careful consideration, is to continue with the program. Get into step four. Ignore the parts of the Bible that are too hard for understanding and pray to my higher power for help. Would I trade all this for the chance to run my own life, be successful, be happy, be able to drink successfully? Probably. But that's just not possible. I know I'm at a crossroads, but I know there is only one way to go. Really.

Day 91, Oct. 28 *(meeting 86)*

A 9.5. Braves win. It really happened. Really. And I was stone-cold sober for every pitch. What a night. What a day. We rode about ten miles on our bikes. Ate a great lunch. Washed the car. Just lived. I just prayed for strength and if it was God's will that the Braves lose, I could accept it. And they won. THEY WON. Now, if only I hadn't let Bandit, our ferret, out of the bedroom window by accident. . . .

I picked up a three-month chip tonight. Praise God for all his gifts.

Day 92, Oct. 29 (meeting 87)
A 6. Nothing worked at work. I slept little after the Braves won, got up at 7:30 for church. Went to some cheerleading competition for the kids. Went to work. I'm dead. But these things don't bother me anymore. Look at this: Carrie's softball team won the championship; Shanna's all-star team won the district and went to state. Our team finished second by one game. The Braves won the World Series. I quit drinking, really quit. I lost fifty-plus pounds. Mary lost twenty-five pounds. What a year.

Thanksgiving should be a long one.

CHAPTER 10

Father Dearest

*As a father has compassion on his children,
so the Lord has compassion on those who fear him.*
—Psalms 103: 13

It was a Sunday afternoon. Spring. The honeysuckle bushes that sweeten the community of Lizelia (community as in four or five houses, no stores, no post office; more cows than humans, but no farms) were in full working order.

Daddy told me to wash my car and his. He was working in his shop, a building he'd constructed one hundred feet out from the house on the hill we knew as home. He'd gotten some huge, old tin signs with Miller High Life painted on them and used them as sheathing for walls, nailing them to posts. He put his various tools, contraptions, junk out there. When he wasn't traveling as an iron worker, which he did for many years, he often worked at projects in his shop. He kept a bottle of whiskey out there at all times. I found it once when I was looking for that old knife he'd given me that looked so much like Tarzan's.

This particular Sunday, he had started out in a good mood. His moods often went the way of the wind, or the way of the bottle. I can't remember a day he was around that he didn't drink. Maybe my memory is bad. Maybe that's the way I want to remember it, since my disgust and dislike of him were so great. I don't know, but I do know that on this day, he drifted into a rage. Why? Who can say? Ostensibly, it was because I didn't wash the cars the way he wanted me to. Probably I didn't. I never did anything the way he wanted me to. It became a running joke in the family. We'd argue about whether it was day or night.

This Sunday, however, he crossed the line for the first time, though not for the last. He walked to me in a rush, took his false teeth out (which he always did when he was ready to fight), and pushed me against one of the cars, ripping one of my favorite shirts. I did nothing. I was sixteen, a junior in high school. I weighed in the neighborhood of one hundred and thirty-five pounds. He was six feet, two inches of power. He screamed at me, the spittle flying. Questioned how I could be his son. Called me a name I'd heard on the football field to describe the genitals of a woman.

I did nothing, did not talk back, did not fight back. I couldn't. Fear had frozen me.

Finally, his point made in his mind, he staggered back to his shop.

I watched him go, beyond mad. When I calmed down to being merely enraged, I walked into the house. I took the keys to his truck, the keys to the family car, and my keys from the rack near the telephone. I smiled at Mama who saw me do this but said nothing, not knowing what had happened. I walked out to my car, cranked it, made a loud circle on the grass-covered parking space out behind the house and punched the car into second as I straightened and headed for the gravel driveway. In the rearview mirror I could see Daddy come running out of the shop, and through the side mirror I could see Mama exiting the back door to the house. Maybe she had figured something out. Maybe she was just reacting to the noise. I never asked.

I poured the gas to the engine and roared down the drive to the rise at the end that intersected with Highway 39. I had decided I was going to my aunt's house in Brooklyn.

I was running away. It was not the first time I'd run away from a problem, and would certainly not be the last. But I was running away from him for the first time. I didn't understand until about five months into recovery that I'd been running to him all my life.

✦ ✦ ✦

When Daddy was about to undergo surgery for cancer for the first time, I was there. I prayed for him, probably for the first time in twenty years, in the hospital chapel. I prayed for forgiveness for the animosity that had been between him and me for all those years. It had gotten better in the last years of his life. Grandchildren and losing his health seemed to finally calm whatever ills had caused him to be who he was.

Mama told me he had found Christ and had quit drinking and smoking two years before his death. He and Aunt Bernece had become close. She'd ministered to him, and he'd accepted Christ as his savior.

I hated that. Just hated it. He'd treated his own son like dirt for all those years, and now he said he was going to heaven. Where was the justice in that?

In mid-afternoon of a November day in 1981, he was lying on a gurney, about to go into surgery. Mama was crying softly, standing to the side as Aunt Bernece talked to that huge man. His stomach had turned almost yellow and its girth was purely embarrassing. His legs were thin, his arms withered. But his stomach had pumped up as the liver began to quit. He was going in for exploratory surgery, they told us. I had no idea he was beginning to die.

Aunt Bernece comforted him. I remember him saying softly that he loved Jesus and thanking her for what she'd done for him. He was scared of dying. Scared of the pain he was already beginning to feel. Mama walked over, kissed his stubbly check. She squeezed his hand and told him we'd be waiting when he woke up.

I, the only child and heir, took his limp hand and held it. I told him I loved him. I meant it. With everything else that he was, he was still my father, the only one I'd ever known.

I waited for him to say he loved me. Whisper it. Shout it. Scream at me as he always used to do. Tell me he loved me as he once told me he'd kill me—just before I broke two of his ribs with a left hook (I was twenty-five and he'd just put Jason down). Tell me he loved me as he once told me he'd break my teeth; just before he punched, I ducked, and he broke his hand.

Tell me he liked me, even.

Tell me Dad. I was waiting. I wasn't doing a darn thing wrong. I wasn't arguing, not any more. I had quit fighting. I wasn't doing anything but staring at a dying man.

Just waiting.

I thought I'd always be waiting.

✦ ✦ ✦

You can waste a lifetime searching for the whys. Why did this have to happen? Why did that have to happen?

I haven't an idea why my life has played out as it has. But as I got deeply into step four of the Alcoholics Anonymous program, it occurred to me that examining it could be healing.

For the first time, I asked my mother about my early life. I was born in 1953, in Meridian, Mississippi, at St. Joseph's Hospital. I was two months premature and almost died. Because of the premature birth, I had physical problems that would require several surgeries over the years, ironically at the same hospital where I would later receive treatment for alcoholism.

My birth mother was a very young teacher with the last name of Carroll or Carol, who lived in Georgia. She had family in a little community south of Meridian. My birth father is totally unknown, at least by Mama. Maybe because of the impending surgery bills or because she was unwed, my birth mother gave me up for adoption.

Daddy and Mama had been married for seven years without having a child; thus they were looking for one they could adopt. Mama heard about me when I was three months old, and the adoption was facilitated by the hospital. My name was changed from Peter to William, after my adoptive father.

Daddy came from rough stock, miners from West Virginia. They apparently were very poor. I know little about the family. For a while we went there every Christmas, but that slowed down and finally stopped in 1969. Dad's family began dying off; all are gone except for a sister in Florida.

He worked away from home a lot, and he drank when he was home. I know he liked to play cards. He was good with his tough, callused hands, good at building things, working on cars.

I know he liked sports, and I guess I got that from him. The only points of communication that we had, as I recall, involved sports. He was a Yankees fan, and he loved the New Orleans Saints. I prayed all the final year of his life for the Saints to win the Super Bowl for him, but it didn't happen.

Kids, no matter what is done to them, no matter what they miss, still love their parents. I'm convinced of it. We might hate them at times, but the bit of love that is unconditional stays firm.

He was a racist, raised in the times. He was sexist. He was old-fashioned and conservative. He voted Democrat, because he was union above all else. The iron workers' union was his religion.

He didn't go to church, didn't care for "those" people. He never threw a ball with me, never really understood what I chose to do for a living. To my knowledge, he never taught me a single thing.

And yet, and yet, the funeral home was filled with sweet

flowers and sweeter people when he died. It was crammed. The book they give you, with the signatures of those who have come to view the dead, was filled.

That bothered me, too. It still makes me wonder.

Didn't these people know how he could be? Didn't they know what he'd done to me? Didn't they understand that he could drive Mama mad?

✦ ✦ ✦

It's 1964. Summer. Dad is working in Vicksburg, Mississippi, on some new plant they're building. We own a neat Chevrolet Impala, canary yellow with a black vinyl top. A 327 V-8 positioned nicely under the hood. Dad drives it. Mom and I go to visit in an old Ford during the week. We usually see him only on the weekends, so this is special.

I'm listening to the radio. It's about six o'clock, and Dad should have been home at five-fifteen. Mama has the beginnings of worry lines appearing near her eyes. The radio is playing "Eight Days a Week," a new Beatles song. Mama puts on a bag of Jiffy Pop popcorn, the first time we've ever bought this. It burns, the stink filling Dad's little rental apartment. Mama airs out the two-room dwelling, and the smoke drifts out into the humid air. Laughter fills the empty rooms. We're happy, happy to be seeing Daddy. Happy to be together.

If he would just get home. Soon.

Daddy arrives about eight, finding two concerned family members. He smells of bourbon, a smell I will come to know. Mama and he start out talking rapidly on the front steps of the apartment. Soon, they're screaming at each other.

Mama and I grab our bags. We drive home to Meridian. Hours on the road.

✦ ✦ ✦

It's 1968. Summer. Best summer of my life. We're playing a rival youth team from a town called Beulah Hubbard at their place. We hear a commotion over by the rest rooms. We discover later that Daddy walked into the women's bathroom. It's late in the game; Daddy is all over the umpire, questioning every call. He's all over me, the catcher, questioning everything I do. The umpire finally has enough, turns to him and tells him that if he doesn't shut up, we will have to forfeit. Daddy doesn't stop. He screams that the umpire has no idea which team he is rooting for. I make sure there can be no doubt by taking off my mask and screaming at Daddy to please, please shut up. I offer him my mitt. Tell him if he can do better, come get it.

Daddy has been drinking, but even then he knows when to shut up.

As I walk away from the field, I hear some fans talking about that motormouth.

✦ ✦ ✦

It's not that I believe that everything that went wrong, that everything I ever did was his fault. So I didn't have this or that. So what?

Mama gave me as much as she could. She still does. That's another story. As the Eagles song says, you have to "get over it" sometime. I still had to grow up and grow spiritually, whatever my childhood was. Maybe on my own, maybe without what the other kids had in a dad. But sooner or later, I had to get over it.

What I missed, however, did affect everything I was.

Gary Smalley and John Trent, the authors of *The Gift of the Blessing*, propose that for years after we move away from home physically, we still remain chained to the past emotionally, that our lack of approval from our parents in the past keeps a feeling of genuine acceptance from others in the present from taking root in our lives. They write, "Some people are driven toward workaholism as they search for the blessing they never received at home. Always striving for acceptance, they never feel satisfied that they are measuring up. Others get mired in withdrawal and apathy as they give up hope of ever truly being blessed. For almost all children who miss out on their parents' blessing, at some level this lack of acceptance sets off a lifelong search."

My relationship with my adoptive father helped make me what I was. I worked extra hours, and was motivated by the desire to have my superiors tell me what a great worker I was. Toward the end, when they didn't, not because of what I did or didn't do but because of the people they were, I drank about it.

Smalley and Trent further wrote, "A family blessing begins with meaningful touching. It continues with a spoken message of high value, a message that pictures a special future for the individual being blessed and one that is an active commitment to see the blessing come to pass."

Strikes one, two, three, and four.

And I was out of the house.

I never got any of that from my father. And Mama can talk all she wants to about how we just didn't love him enough, we just didn't do this or that. The fact remains that we have a job to do as parents. And he failed his.

✦ ✦ ✦

So in doing step four, in looking back, I'd found a little resentment toward my father. I honestly hadn't given him or the past a lot of thought over the years. Mary had never even seen much of this. My fights with him were all but over before I married her. He was a good grandparent, caring and playful with the kids.

I'd buried the thoughts of the worst times in the deepest, darkest parts of my memory.

But they came roaring back when I did step four. With the resentment squarely in front of me, what could I do with it? What part had I played in all of this? I thought, and thought.

And it struck me with the same force Daddy had used all those years ago on me. One night, lying in bed with Mary, journaling in a blue spiral notebook, bits and pieces of memory fell away like the scales off the apostle's eyes.

Had I ever asked him why he drank? Had I ever asked him what made him unhappy? Had I ever asked him why, why, why we had those problems? What if, just what if, he was bothered by the fact that he couldn't have kids? What if, just what if, he took that feeling of inadequacy out on me?

What if he just didn't know where to get help? What if he couldn't, because of an upbringing I knew nothing about, admit his weakness? What if he just was an alcoholic and couldn't help it? Just like me. I knew nothing of his problems. He seemed so big to me, right up to the end of his life, when the very act of taking a breath was a chore.

I do not excuse anything he did, or, more important, didn't do. I believe he kept from me the hug that I wanted more than the car I got when I was fifteen.

What I began to learn was that I had to forgive him, or I would eventually drink again. It was that simple. I would sin like everyone else. But my sin would be one of unforgiveness, which would bring back fresh pangs of guilt, which would eventually lead my hand to a glass.

I'd drink the deep sorrow from the glass. And it would kill me, if not literally, then certainly spiritually. It had once. It would again.

So, through days of tormented effort, I worked on forgiveness. It took two weeks before I could say it and mean it. I prayed for it nightly. I really tried.

✦ ✦ ✦

It's Christmas Day, 1995. I drive Carrie to Papaw's grave that evening. It is blustery and cool. The oaks and elms in the forests outside of Lauderdale—a dusty, aged town north of Meridian—

are in a stage of deep yellow and burnt orange. The changing of the leaves occurs later in the winter in the South. But I believe that the countryside is as beautiful as it must be in New England—not as brilliant, but as nice in its own way.

I drive along the winding, black-topped country road. It'll never see another drop of tar, that's for sure, and now it is shattering with each of the infrequent freezes. I drive past the church with the white siding and dull tin roof on top of the hill above the road. I've never seen any cars nearby, but as long as I can remember the church has been there.

We used to come to this graveyard, a family cemetery maintained by Mama's large group of relatives, to cut grass. I used to play on a big magnolia tree at the entrance to the yard. I remember vividly the huge blossoms that would cover the ground as you walked in.

I drive into the parking area for the first time in five years. The last time I was there, twenty-four young men—all the people in the sports department of the Jackson (Miss.) *Clarion-Ledger*, a newspaper where I worked for ten years—were standing outside that long chain-link fence. They'd come to support me and my family at the funeral.

Carrie and I leave the car running, to keep the heat on, and walk to the front gate. I slip the lock, pull the pole out of the ground, and slide the gate back enough for us to get in. I show her the graves—aunts and uncles, two little cousins we never knew, and on and on. Graves broken by time and shifting earth going back to the 1800s.

I take her to the area to the left of the entrance. There is Dad's grave. William Glenn Turner. Born 1922, died 1989. His middle name is misspelled, actually. But his headstone is shiny, unlike the majority of the ones in this cemetery which are so much older.

There are some plastic flowers slung over the fence, and Carrie asks if we can get one or two, pull them back through the fence, and put them on the grave so he'd have some.

I say of course, and we do.

I ask Carrie if she will give me a second, and she walks quickly back to the car. I know she doesn't understand why we are there. I'm not sure I do either.

I begin slowly, searching for the right words for reasons I can't explain. I still am trying to do the right thing, to say the right thing, to receive his approval.

I want to tell him I turned out just about the way he did. I want to tell him I understand how devious alcohol can be. I want to say that I wish I could have done this years earlier and could have helped him. I want to say so much.

✦ ✦ ✦

I could tell you I cried. I could tell you I felt on top of the world. Neither would be true.

There's a scene in the movie *Field of Dreams* in which Kevin Costner turns and sees his father, young, before he got caught in the storms of life, with a ball and a glove. The father asks a simple question: "Wanna play a game of catch?" Costner smiles, maybe chokes a little, and says sure.

The first time I saw that movie, tears were pouring onto my shirt. The last time I saw the video, tears were pouring onto my shirt.

That day in the cemetery, as the leaves blew across the brown, dead grass, I didn't cry. In fact, my lips drew up into a bit of a smile. I told Dad I'd be seeing him. And I meant it.

That's what faith in Jesus does for you. We'll have a chance to get together again. Maybe we won't get another chance to do this father-son thing right. But that's all right.

I love you, Daddy.

That's what the trip to the cemetery was for. I forgave him. I asked for his forgiveness. And I left it at that.

I never would have had that opportunity if I hadn't quit drinking. I never would have had that opportunity if there were no Father who loves me, who gives me the blessing I seek on a daily basis.

I'm not waiting any longer. I'm loved. And I'm healing.

PART TWO

A Long Day's Journey into Right

CHAPTER 11

Journal 5
October 30-November 29

Day 93, Oct. 30

A 6 or a 7. I got a chip from the home group. I really feel balance today. Things are going my way—that's when it's easy. But if I remember to thank God, don't spend needlessly, accept the gifts I'm given with humility and true gratefulness, things will be fine.

Day 94, Oct. 31

A 4. We sort of lost it at Shanna today. She was late for class, and we overreacted. It's hard being a parent when you're trying to learn to live on your own terms, to grow up yourself.

Day 95, Nov. 1

A 7. I did the best I could. Sometimes, well, most of the time, that's all you have.

Day 96, Nov. 2

A 5. I was and am really tired. But I did a good job at work. Carrie said something interesting today. I told her when I took her to school that I'm happier than I've ever been before. She smiled a gap-toothed grin and said, "Me too, Daddy, except for that time we went back to Meliah's house." That was three years ago when Carrie was six and we went back to visit the little town we'd lived in previously to see friends. If Carrie remembers that so clearly, what must she remember of the times I screamed at her, or passed out on the floor, or drank beer after beer at a ball game?

Day 97, Nov. 3
A great day. An 8. Rainy, cold. Balanced.

Day 98, Nov. 4.
More balance. This is becoming easier. I don't know why or how, but I accept it.

Day 99, Nov. 5
A 3. Not a good day at all. Mary and I fought over prayer, of all things. Over prayer. Carrie was crying about the thought of going to Sunday school by herself, into the class by herself. We'd been working toward this day for a while. So, I backed off and tried to have a little Sunday school here. I told her about Samson, then we began to pray. But as I prayed, Mary kept turning pages of the newspaper loudly. I exploded. Then she exploded, showering me with the feelings she had built up about this whole process. Mostly about how critical I was of her. So, we never made it to church.

I honestly didn't realize I was being critical of her. I didn't realize I was asking her to change at the pace I was trying to change. Heck, I've got enough to worry about, worrying about me.

Day 100, Nov. 6.
They measure presidencies by this amount of time. With me, I only know what I know. Balance, I've come to believe, means taking the bad and pushing through it as if it were a blocking dummy on the football field and also taking the good,

being grateful but not lingering on it. Not too high, not too low. Don't do too much or too little. Praise God for my sobriety, be humble when things are good. I love sobriety. It's a rollercoaster, but at least I got on the ride instead of watching it from the parking lot.

Day 101, Nov. 7

Balanced like that guy on the old Ed Sullivan show, spinning plates. Good balance, but Lord help me if one of the plates falls.

Day 104, Nov. 10

I played the best golf I have played in some time, for one reason, essentially. I got up, had my coffee, smoked outside under a cool sky, and went to the course with little or no expectation. I can see something of what everyone is talking about—living in the moment. If you can focus, bring together the physical and spiritual for just a moment, you can achieve peace. And every once in a great while, you can hit a pitching wedge stiff.

Day 105, Nov. 11

I've felt a restlessness today. A lack of faith or something. I've got this hard-to-describe, hard-to-pinpoint feeling that something is missing, that I'm slipping away. I went to meetings yesterday and today because of that feeling. A little Allstate for the alcoholic. I'm scared that I feel cured and I'll stop doing the things I need to do to make it keep going. I need to stop and think about whether I am doing everything I can for my spirituality and my sobriety.

Day 107, Nov. 13

A 4. My head is killing me. But even while I was stressed, rushed and pulled today—as I did my boss's job as well as my own because he is on vacation—I learned. I prayed for patience. I prayed to be able to see each task and work at it one at a time.

I couldn't find some pictures I needed and I asked God to clear my head enough to remember where I put them. And he did. Honest.

Day 108, Nov. 14

I finished step 4, except for some review to make sure I didn't forget something. Maybe I'll write about the mom and dad I never knew. I did go to the doctor, so maybe the head pain will go away.

Day 109, Nov. 15

I need to work on some things in my program and in my life, among them getting back to exercise, controlling spending with Mary's input, being disciplined about eating, actively pursuing humility, actively pursuing doing things with the kids, whether it's playing games or whatever. I've slipped in my orderly day some. Time to get going again.

I talked to my sponsor for about an hour, and I believe I am turning from a disgruntled person worried about my faith, into a much more faithful person. I know this: I don't have to try and understand God. I will or I won't. If I open my heart, it will come. If I open my head and try to understand, I might never have the relationship I want. I've got to learn to love. How the heck do you do that?

Day 110, Nov. 16

We had a Bible study group tonight and I shared some of my experience. It wasn't too bad. I even felt that I was somewhat accepted. I know they can't completely empathize, but they accepted. I was happy to share with humility my weakness but also to look for the strength of Jesus.

Day 111, Nov. 17

A wonderful weekend awaits. Decisions everywhere. Here's where I try: God grant me an understanding of what you want me to do. I feel this inner happiness that's very hard to describe. I want to do things for others, more than ever before in my life. How? That's for God to let me know.

"Let us draw near to God with a sincere heart in full assurance of faith, having our hearts sprinkled to cleanse us from a guilty conscience and having our bodies washed with pure water."

I learned some things today. Let God in, don't try to force Him in. None of the good things I want for my life will come from anything I do. That's so hard to understand. They are gifts. And I've never accepted gifts very well. I believe my problems are immense. What if I can never completely surrender? Some people must be better at it than others. What if I'm no good at it? What if I can't change? All I've changed has been the direction of my efforts, not the inner being.

I'll keep trying, I hope, but part of me really wants to say to heck with all this. It's too hard to understand, too hard to do.

Day 112, Nov. 18

Very important to understand: In whatever degree any man or woman is obedient to the will of God, that is the degree of joy he or she will experience here and now. As Christ alone did God's will perfectly, so was his joy perfect.

Now that I understand that, if I can just get a little grasp on what God's will for me is, I got this licked.

Day 117, Nov. 23

Interesting. A holiday. Alone. Sober. Mary and the kids went to Mama's. I stayed because I had to work. I cleaned house and prayed a lot. I didn't feel I moved in God's will too well. I don't know why. I recognize the level of my spiritual maturity. So I let go and let God in again. When will it become a habit, a way of life instead of a thing I must try to do? But through it all, this is better than before. I can remember practically every day of the past four months and almost all of them have been happy ones. What's wrong with sitting, listening to classical music (my new love) in a clean house, getting restful sleep, staying sober? It's what many drunks would kill for. And I have it. But when that grace of God hits you, that's the special moment I want to call mine all of the time. I believe everything that's good in my life comes from God, a true gift. I just have to accept it—then try to do his will. Sounds easy; it's not. I am ever more human. And I make so many mistakes. But I'm trying. Why don't I get better at it?

Day 118, Nov. 24

"When I applied my mind to know wisdom and to observe man's labor on earth—his eyes not seeing sleep day or night—than I saw all that God has done. No one can comprehend what goes on under the sun. Despite all his efforts to search it out, man cannot understand its meaning." (Ecclesiastes 8: 16-17)

What gives me joy: 1) cool weather; 2) baseball, both youth and major leagues; 3) my kids' smiles; 4) a clean house; 5) a roaring fire, hot coffee, and Mary laughing beside me; 6) early mornings, coffee steaming in a mug, a Kool, and contemplation; 7) a good sports section or a good book; 8) music; 9) the bit of grace God gives me when I feel the warmth inside, the peace, the purpose.

Day 119, Nov. 25

I wrote a story for Carrie's Christmas. It came to me and wrote itself. I hadn't been able to write for years. It took time, time away from my pity parties.

Day 120, Nov. 26

Worry creeps back to the corner of my mind. Christmas is coming. We're paying off many of the overdue bills, but we have so very little cash for Christmas. I don't worry about myself, but I do for the kids. My journey hasn't gone that far that the material things don't matter. And I know they still matter to Mary and the kids. I pray for strength and God's help in this matter.

Day 121, Nov. 27

My sponsor gave me a book, *Walking with Christ in the Details of Life*. That sure helped me to understand some of this walk with Christ. I've gone away from some of the teachings of AA. I believe, and my sponsor agrees, that Christ is the only answer. I don't think he was kidding in the Bible.

Day 122, Nov. 28

What would keep me from following Christ? From *Walking with Christ in the Details of Life*: "It is trusting him to produce the spiritual life in us, not trusting in ourselves to produce the spiritual life by our own effort." I believe that means that all this effort I've put into my spirituality is not as necessary as I thought. I acknowledge the gift.

Father, I confess that I have wanted to be remembered by men. I have been making plans and asking you to bless them. I know these plans are doomed to fail. I surrender my plans to you.

Day 123, Nov. 29

"I urge you to live a life worthy of the calling you have received." (Ephesians 4: 1)

In other words, I can't plan my spiritual progress. I can reflect on the gift in gratitude; I can look at where my slips have been and ask God for more strength and courage in those areas. But none of this comes completely from effort. My best efforts got me drunk and dead spiritually. My best efforts won't save me.

I need to slow down even more, I believe. I need to find even more humility, more prayer for humility. I can't make myself humble. God has blessed me with a little ability in some areas; I should thank him, but not use those abilities to harm others or belittle others.

I went to a 10:30 p.m. meeting tonight and shared my complete surrender. And felt the true peace of God come over me. Somehow, this whole idea has taken root in me. Jesus told us that those who lose their life gain their life. I think I'm beginning to understand that he wasn't talking about dying. He was describing the complete surrender that one must have in order to grow.

Thank you, Jesus, for the wisdom that the seed of the Word has begun to grow.

Heaven knows I didn't do it.

At least I've come that far.

CHAPTER 12

Ch-Ch-Ch-Changes

*So come to me, all you who are weary
and burdened, and I will give you rest.
Take my yoke upon you and learn from me,
for I am gentle and humble.*
—Matthew 11: 28-30

Just as I ran away literally from my father when I was sixteen, I had been figuratively running away from my Father for many years.

As the days of sobriety turned into months, I tried my very best to run back to him, somehow understanding through the teachings of AA that this was my only chance to live the kind of life I wanted.

As late summer turned into fall and then winter came, I tried. I tried more than anyone I knew associated with the program. I journaled in the morning, prayed, read from *The Big Book* and read from the Bible, even began to read books on spirituality.

I finished the evening with prayer, half-hearted and unsuccessful meditation, more journaling, more verses from the Bible.

I talked spirituality at meetings. I asked questions. I listened. I shared more than others at meetings, already understanding that in helping others I would inevitably help myself.

And what I found was a wall, a veritable fortress around God. A mountain I could not climb.

✦ ✦ ✦

Our dog Goofy was a stray. On a bright August morning during the first year we were in New Orleans, Carrie was waiting outside the apartment we'd rented as we tried to save money to get back into a home of our own. A small mixed-breed dog walked up to Carrie, licked her hand, and sat down beside her. Carrie, whose love for animals is surprising considering that when a German shepherd rearranged some of her face she was three (the scars are still slightly visible), petted the little short-haired blonde dog.

Carrie asked immediately if the dog could stay. As the bus chugged into sight, I said I'd think about it if the dog was still there when Carrie came back from school. Of course, the dog was still there. Carrie, who has named most of our animals, chose the name Goofy.

Goofy stayed with us through the addition of Scrappy, a peekapoo mix that we saved from the animal shelter right before Christmas a year and a half later. She stayed with us through the addition of Boomer, a shepherd mix that we saved from a gas station bathroom on the interstate.

But when Boomer grew into a much, much larger dog and began to pick on Goofy, Goofy didn't stay. She simply left. She'd had enough.

She knew when change was necessary. And through some unseen, unheard call (of the tame and spoiled), she packed her little doggie bag (small ball, a couple of dog biscuits for the road), and left.

Change wasn't difficult for her. She loved me, I know. She grew to put up with Carrie, who dressed her in doll's clothing and bought her a red collar Goofy detested. She put up with Scrappy's puppy playing, which Goofy was much too mature to like. She learned to stay away from Buttons and Squeeker (the cats), who really couldn't stand Goofy, but seemed to like Scrappy.

But when Boomer began to guard the food with growls, Goofy could tell. The clock in her aged brain told her to change. Her little body complied. The wall she had to scale was a six-foot wooden fence.

Like Steve McQueen in *The Great Escape*, Goofy planned. She began slowly, digging through the soil for enough space to slip underneath the fence. Then she'd wait by the front door for our return, with, I swear, a grin on her face.

I bought cement, and began to apply it in strips to the bottom of the fence. She made other holes.

Always she'd be waiting by the front door, hoping this time we'd get the message and would allow her the run of the house, as she'd had before Scrappy, and Boomer, before we built the fence and moved the dogs into the backyard.

Eventually the call for change led her to burrow her way to freedom, pull her stuff through the hole with her and leave. Without so much as a message, Goofy was gone. We've never seen her since. Not a card. Not a letter. Not a call. Just gone.

She saw the need for change, constructed a plan, refused to be stopped by the mountain in front of her, acted upon the plan, and got what she wanted. I thought I could do the same, but I was wrong.

I'm not an animal. My needs are much deeper, my resolve not as strong. And my mountain was much higher.

✦ ✦ ✦

There's a story about Siddhartha, a boy who seeks God. He asks anyone and everyone who he thinks can help him to give instruction. Eventually, he hears of a special teacher who lives alone, high in the mountains. It is said that this teacher knows more about God than any other teacher or prophet.

Siddhartha goes to him, and asks the simple question: How can I find God?

The teacher does not immediately answer. Instead, he asks Siddhartha to follow him. He leads the boy to the edge of the lake, and then, unexpectedly and violently, grabs Siddhartha's head and shoves it under water.

Siddhartha tries to escape but can't. Even when the strength that comes from the panic of nearly drowning sets in, he cannot break the teacher's hold. Just when it seems his lungs will burst and his life will end, the teacher pulls Siddhartha's head from the water. As the boy is about to cry out against the guru for what has been done to him, the teacher raises his hand for silence. Then he says softly, "When you want God as much as you have just wanted breath, you'll find Him."

✦ ✦ ✦

That was my mountain. I wanted God, needed God, couldn't accept not hearing God. Although I was learning to see God's work in sunsets and tall, majestic trees, in fluffy white clouds, and in the dramatic crash of thunder before downpours, I wanted more. I always did. I wanted an intimacy. I wanted a discourse. I wanted Him to talk to me when I prayed. I wanted to know His will.

His yoke is easy, Jesus said. So why, oh, why was I struggling like a caught fish?

I had cut my hair shorter than it had been since high school, parted it on the opposite side, lost over fifty pounds, learned to exercise for the first time when there wasn't a score involved. I'd changed habits, friendships, appearance. I'd done everything I was told to do.

I wanted the applause of heaven. I wanted blessings right there and then, at my demand. I was putting new wine into an old wineskin as fast as I could pour it.

I was spoiled, acting like Goofy, who wanted to be fed, and

given water when she wanted it, wanted the rest of the world at her beck and call. If she couldn't have it that way, she'd run away.

And, toward Thanksgiving, the idea passed through my mind at times. If I couldn't make this work, this God thing, if doubts crept in like thieves after midnight, I would fail. I couldn't accept failure this time.

The mountain was slippery, the valley so far below me, and the climbing had been exhausting. I was on a precipice; one slip would be the end, I thought.

And I came across this in the daily devotions connected with the Recovery Bible. "At this point in our program, we see that change is necessary to live life to the fullest. Recognizing the need for change and being willing to change are two different matters. The space between recognition and willingness can be filled with fear. As we move toward willingness, we must let go of our fears and remain secure in the knowledge that with God's guidance everything will be restored to us." (*Friends in Recovery*)

Certainly I wanted to change. That was the whole point. But how? In answer, God slapped me in the head and made it clear to me. It was not the first time; it would not be the last.

As I slipped tired hand up and over tired hand, inching my way up the citadel wall that I could see surrounding God, God reached down, gave me a warm, loving hand, and helped me up.

✦ ✦ ✦

M. Scott Peck, whose book *The Road Most Traveled* is one of the best books on spiritual growth on the market, wrote the following: "I have come to believe that people's capacity to love, and hence their will to grow, is nurtured not only by the love of their parents during childhood but also throughout their lives by grace, or God's love. This is a powerful external force which operates through their own unconscious as well as through loving persons other than their parents and through additional ways which we do not understand. It is because of grace that it is possible for people to transcend the traumas of loveless parenting and become themselves far more loving individuals than their parents.

"Why, then, do only some people spiritually grow and mature beyond the circumstances of their parentage? I believe that grace is available to everyone, that we are all cloaked in the love of God, no one less nobly than another. The only answer I can give, therefore, is that most of us choose not to heed the call of grace and to reject its assistance. I would translate Christ's assertion 'Many are invited, but few are chosen' to mean 'All of us are called by and to grace, but few of us choose to listen to the call.' "

The problem I had, the mountain I kept screaming at as being too large for my efforts, was me.

Plain. Simple.

Me.

I couldn't get out of the way.

Whatever was in me that made me successful in business, whatever I had learned at the knee of an alcoholic about being a man, about doing the job, whatever I had learned at the knees of father substitutes (my coaches) over the years wouldn't let me not do this myself.

I had gotten myself in this position; I could get myself out. With the right effort, the right works, the right thoughts, the right actions. I could do it. I now knew the correct way to live. I understood most of it. I had a plan, a course of action, motivation.

And the mountain grew larger every day—the mountain of guilt, the mountain of stress, the mountain of bills, the mountain of parentage, the mountain of the past, the present, the future. The harder I struggled, the larger the mountain grew.

There were also mountains of depression, of grief, of anger, of resentment, of cursing, of smoking, all the character faults I was being told had to be taken away by God. And where was

God? Silent when I asked for help in prayer, as far as I could tell.

But his hand wasn't far. I just couldn't see it, my eyes being so dimmed by the shadow of the mountain I perceived to be unclimbable.

✦ ✦ ✦

It is a Friday night, late October, 1995. I go to an AA meeting at the Camel Club. It is a candlelight meeting. I arrive early, clean the table of ashes from the many trays. I put on a pot of regular coffee and one of decaf. I take little plastic stirring straws, light the end of one at a time and place them on the wicks of candles in little jars.

People arrive almost exactly at 10:30 p.m., coming from in back where they gather on the weekends to shoot pool, play cards, watch TV or just talk. I never joined the club, nor spent much time in the back, though I don't know why.

We begin the meeting in the usual manner, with the announcements, the reading of the portion of the fifth chapter of *The Big Book*, and the serenity prayer.

Then we cut the lights off.

Sometime during that meeting, the lights finally go on for me.

We go around the room, sharing. As God would have it, I am near the end of the progression. I halfheartedly listen to what is being said. It is basically the same people saying the same things I have heard for months. The subject that night is step three, making a decision to turn your will over to God as you understand Him.

But I'd done that the first week of treatment. I have no reason to be listening to this again. I want more. I want meat instead of milk. I have read more than all these people combined. I've done more praying, more writing, more introspection. Their pitiful little stories aren't as good as mine. What am I doing there?

When it comes time to share, boy, do I share. I tell them just what I think, what I feel. I question what we are doing, what the purpose of all this is.

Let's get logical, I tell them. If God wants me to do something, and I want to do it, why not come right out and tell me? "I'm trying to do His will, I promise," I say, exasperation and a trembling fear lingering in my tone. "If it can be tried, I've done it. And I feel no closer to God than I did a month ago." I ramble, I rave. At times I come close to shouting.

Finally, I wrap it up with the usual "Thank you for letting me share." I say it with a tone of monotony. I am not thankful at all. There isn't a shred of gratitude in me.

Thank God for Ida.

She is sitting next to me. The last of the night to share, Ida is smoking a long, thin cigarette and sipping on a cup of decaf. She listens to me with a smile. She introduces herself, as is the custom at AA, and instead of talking about herself she talks about me.

She says it's okay to feel the way I do. She says I am right where God wants me. She says that God is allowing me to exhaust myself trying to fix myself before I finally, without breath and without a clue as to where to go next, look up instead of inside. She says she knows because she'd taken the same path. She'd even gone back to college to study religion. And what she found she will offer freely to me if I will listen, she says.

In a quiet setting, shadows from the candles flickering on the walls, a cup of tepid coffee in front of me, I hear (really hear for the first time) the words that would really begin to produce the change in me that I'd been trying for so hard.

"This is about love. God's love for you, not your love for God, Billy," Ida says. "You can't impress Him. You can't win Him over. There's not a game to be won here. God loves you no matter what you do or don't do. He always has. Whatever you've done in the past, He forgives you. I see forgiveness as the whole picture of His love. He forgives you, not for what you are, who you are, what you do or don't do. He forgives you and loves you because you are you. Just get out of the way and let Him love you."

✦ ✦ ✦

She said much more, spoke longer than we normally do at those things, stretched the hour toward midnight. But I heard only that much, really. God wiped the slate clean at that moment.

In the dark, in a place where many church members wouldn't be caught dead, I surrendered to Jesus. I willingly gave up my life in order to find it. Willingly. That's the key that M. Scott Peck uses to open the door. It's what's wrong in the story of Siddhartha. Siddhartha wanted to find God, but he wasn't willing to let God find him. It was what was wrong with Goofy's plans. She ran away from the ones who could shelter her and feed her and toward who knows what? Change for her might have meant death.

But the hand that reached down from the top of the mountain for me was a loving one. Where I couldn't take myself, God took me.

CHAPTER 13

Journal 6
December 1 — January 3

Day 125, Dec. 1
Christ Jesus month. My fifth month, beginning.

Bible verse of the day: "Do not judge, or you too will be judged. For in the same way you will judge others, you will be judged and with the same measure you use, it will be measure to you."

Meditation: The remedy for judging: Taking our own moral inventory and asking God to remove our planks.

Tough day, tougher night. Work was terrible. We blew three deadlines, badly. I believe we were too ambitious. Things went from bad to worse.

I am troubled by some of this stuff, and I don't know how much is justified and how much is self-centered. Again, I'll pray about it. It helps me to focus.

Dec. 126, Dec. 2
I've got to reach a point where positive energy radiates—to be positive even if I don't feel that way all the time. I have to ask what the positive way to approach the problem is, instead of why these things are so wrong.

Today was a 7. Primarily because I continue to learn and grow. For two days I've had a burning desire to buy a computer. I would call it a BIG present to the family for Christmas. God tried to put all sorts of obstacles in my way to show it wasn't His will. But I ignored them all. I wanted the rush of a major purchase. Until finally He simply did not let me get a new credit card. And I feel good about it. I surrender all. I didn't get my way and it feels good. Whodathunk it? I do it His way and I get the best gift of all—serenity. I won't be able to get the kids all I would like, but He will provide enough. And maybe they'll learn the true meaning of Christmas. We will find a way to give more to the needy. And I, for one, will celebrate my savior's birth without worry, but with love.

Day 127, Dec. 3

May God himself, the God of peace, sanctify you through and through. May your whole spirit, soul, and body be kept blameless.

A near perfect evening of work. The design work was delightful.

Day 128, Dec. 4

"If calamity comes upon us, whether the sword of judgment or plague or famine, we will stand in your presence before this temple that bears your name and will cry out to you in our distress and you will hear us and save us." (2 Chronicles: 20)

From *Jesus, CEO*, a book I bought at the newspaper's book sale: "Great leaders inspire others to the extent that they inspire themselves . . . When you are surrounded by the state of grace where nothing else matters except the feeling you have within yourself, that is your intersection with destiny."

A very good day. Perhaps it was overwhelming, for I had too much on my plate, especially at work. But God let me get most—if not all—of it done. As he will tomorrow, by faith. Jim Rice and his wife, Tammie, had a baby boy. A healthy baby boy. It takes me back.

But I have a second chance to make it up to my kids.

Day 129, Dec. 5
"Be still before the Lord, all mankind, because he has roused himself from His holy dwelling." (Zechariah 2:13)
Work was as difficult as I imagined. Maybe that's the key. I built it into a difficult thing. And it became one. Self-fulfilling prophecy. I was the problem, not necessarily the work or the circumstances. I made me—my wants, the self-centeredness that is Billy—the center, and that pulled me away from God's sweet grace. I can't worry about whether I'm working more than other assistants. That's not my problem. I have more than enough to worry about on my own terms.

Day 130, Dec. 6
"But the one who hears my words and does not put them into practice is like a man who built a house on the ground without a foundation."
Do the work without reservation, without holding back. God gave me a good, high-paying job. Do I reward Him by not giving my best? I don't think that's a very good idea, upon reflection.

Day 131, Dec. 7
"Where then does wisdom come from? Where does understanding dwell? It is hidden from the eyes of every living thing..." (Ecclesiastes 7: 11-14)
Bandit, our little ferret, is gone. Nothing much more needs to be said. I loved him. He was fun. But he sneaked out the door and is gone. I pray he's all right. I hope he pleases whoever found him. I need to pause and let the Holy Spirit refill me.
11:20: Bandit is still gone. He was a highlight of my recovery. He was playful, fun and smarter than you would give something that looks like a long rat a chance of being.
God allowed me to buy some gifts for the kids and Mom. Praise Him who gives us these ideas. I'm not going to be able to

do all I would like—but enough and Carrie wants money to buy presents, not get them. So things aren't bad. Not at all.

Day 132, Dec. 8
Do I join the church? Is this the one? Does it interfere with AA meetings, or the other way around? I must think on this.

Day 133, Dec. 9
Jason's seventeenth birthday. I understand I'm making a spiritual journey. I'm only a little way along the road. I'm not ready, not capable of giving enough, surrendering enough yet. That's not a failure of mine, or the program, or of my faith, or of my God. I just need to slow down, breathe deeply of the breath that God gives. Take it easy. Take it one step, one day at a time. Love God with all that I have—at the moment. I can't do anything about the past, the lost marriage or the loss of Jason. I can't do anything to hurry my recovery along. The future is promised to absolutely no one. I can only live as hard and as well as I can in this moment, this day. I am where I need to be, and when it's time, I'll grow. I'll quit smoking. I hope I don't die before that moment comes, however.

"I sought the Lord and he answered me; He delivered me from all my fears; those who look to him are radiant, their faces are never covered with shame." (Psalms 34: 4-5)

I can't be perfect.

I can't be perfect.

I can try to be the best I can be.

I can look to God for the help, but perfection was saved for one man.

"We can live ourselves into right thinking but we can't think ourselves into right living." *A New Pair of Glasses* by Chuck C.

Chuck C., a recovering alcoholic who wrote a very helpful book, describes the golden key to life as: "When I perform according to the best I know, there seems to be a nod of approval. The Golden Key is rigorous self-honesty." He defines sobriety as being "the ability to live comfortably, peacefully and joyously with me."

I have learned other things from this book, the best I've read about sobriety and the search for spirituality: "You lose yourself in life and find yourself in God. If you are not as close to God as you once were, or as you would like to be, make no mistake about it, you are the one that moved. If you love someone or something, you do something for them. You just do something for them, and you don't make a big deal out of it. The definition of love is action."

I'm either going to run my life and suffer the consequences or I'm not going to run my life and take the wonderful blessings thereof. I don't know why it was such a hard thing to understand.

There was such understanding and wisdom in that book. I guess God put it in my hands at just the right time. You know, the only thing you can do in life is live it. Being all you can be, in today, is the only thing that counts.

What an absolutely wonderful day.

Day 134, Dec. 10
Today let me have the understanding of God's will for me and the power to carry it out. That's all, folks.

Day 135, Dec. 11
A nice day of work. I helped some people, thanked some people. I love to see the surprise on their faces when I do something they don't expect, like be kind.

"Come, all you who are thirsty come to the waters; and you who have no money come buy and eat; come, buy wine and milk without money and without cost." (Isaiah 55)

Day 137, Dec. 13
Remember, this is a long, long road. I have experienced the grace of God, not for what I did but for what he is. There is no

all or nothing anymore, only degrees. I want to love all, do this perfectly, but it's the striving, the journey that is important, not necessarily the results. If any action I take can make God take just a second to smile at what I did, not to give me salvation but just to please Him, I count it a day well done, even if things were bad.

Day 138, Dec. 14

How about this: When things go wrong, thank God for the pain. It is the touchstone of spiritual progress. I read that somewhere. I must be making progress. I'm sick. I'm very tired. But because of my faith, I know this will pass. Or it won't. Nothing I can do about it.

Day 139, Dec. 15

Bible study journaling:

"We're talking about the promises of God. The unbreakable, the unmistakable promises of God, of which the greatest was our savior's birth. Why spend our time on anything else? Why waste our money on things that do not nourish the soul? Why do jobs that do not help others? The rich promise of God will fill your every need, not want. And it says we will be endowed with splendor. And that is all we should think about, not how many Christmas gifts or how many bills or how many anything. I will go my way in joy and be led forth in peace. That is overpoweringly wonderful. This is a loving God that I have to trust in. I believe in Him and His promises. And have no wants because of that. I know He is near us tonight."

We're joining the church on Jan. 14. I believe that is the perfect thing to do. The Holy Spirit continues to make Himself known to me and is leading us somewhere. I know it. Mary knows it. This is wonderful.

Day 139, Dec. 15

I need to remember to take quiet time, to relax. Seems I'm

struggling on Fridays. The time off, I don't know what it is. I need to have quiet time that I just can't find. And my serenity, which is so dear to me, is affected because of it. I confronted the feeling of disquietness with little prayers for help. I fought the depression that came so suddenly. I survived.

Remember: When pride comes, then comes disgrace; but with humility comes wisdom.

Day 140, Dec. 16

"Whoever loves discipline, loves knowledge, but he who hates correction is stupid." (Proverbs 12: 1)

Just call me stupid. I've never, ever, loved discipline. I pray for it, with utter disgust. I'm sure God gets a real laugh out of it, too.

Day 141, Dec. 17

Lesson learned. I was horrible today. I lost my temper at work. Several times, really. Once outwardly. I was just horrible, without the first clue as to what was wrong.

Then Mary called to tell me Bandit had been found, is doing well and is home.

A miracle any way you view it.

Day 142, Dec. 18

Bandit was a direct answer to a prayer. I was embarrassed to have nothing to put in the collection plate at church. I had money to pay for presents for my kids. I've almost missed the season because of so much work.

I've got to examine my motives. I'm doing some good stuff, but why?

Day 144, Dec. 20

A short night of sleep. Physically, I feel good. Some of the excitement, the energy is coming back. Spiritually, I feel down, distant, less enthusiastic. Relationally, the worst. I don't know how or why but my trust of people is at a low ebb.

Day 145, Dec. 21

I'm worried about step five tonight. My gosh, what if this doesn't work? Don't go by my feelings, they say. Started over on the Bible today. Physically: I ate too much and stayed up too late; spiritually: I feel empty; emotionally: relaxed; relationally: real good with the family.

Why?
Why is this Christmas different?
Not in the obvious,
not in the fewer gifts under the tree;
not in the way we're broke.
Not having our wants met;
not in the temperature or the skies,
through full moon or gray or blue.
It's in the faces—and the hearts;
in the eyes, bright and happy.
It's in the way we know
we're finally—finally—a family,
equal in love and friendship.
Not in the lacking, of which we may
be full as a stomach after a meal.
But in the have
which we did not notice when I drank.
I have, where I wanted.
We have, where we didn't.
Why?
I haven't a clue.
I just know we're blessed to be together.
As a child was born to us on this night
so has our family been born again.
Fresh, beautiful, alive. Together.
Why?
Don't ask. Just thank God, it's true.
I do.

Amazing. I was feeling awful earlier. At another bottom. Then my sponsor led me through steps five, six and seven. I got home and we had won a fifty-dollar gift certificate from Toys R Us on the radio.

It's 2 a.m. From the coffee and what has happened today, I can't sleep.

What a five-month period this has been. What a year. All the things that have gone wrong and all the many things that have gone so very right. I can never repay the hurt I caused, nor can I repay the help I've received. Strange how things turn out.

Day 146, Dec. 22

Ugh. Tired. Sleepy.

"Let us not give up meeting together, as some are in the habit of doing. But let us encourage one another and all the more as you see the day approaching" (Hebrews 10: 25).

Day 147, Dec. 23

Physically: good, a little sleepy and I need to watch my sleeping patterns. Spiritually: okay. Not as centered as two days ago, but good. Emotionally: a little down about how much money we have, or don't have. Relationally: really good.

"But by the grace of God I am what I am, and his grace to me was not without effect." (1 Corinthians 15: 10)

It is cold, flat-out cold. I think I froze cleaning out the van. Jason is down and we opened some gifts.

Day 148, Dec. 24

It's 3 a.m. Stoked on caffeine and meetings, I am awake. I want to remember this Christmas. We've been out of money basically the whole month. We didn't buy many gifts, but I promise this is the best Christmas ever. I don't want to be this broke again, but this is a valuable experience. We've hung together; we've not lost the love I've always wanted to see at

Christmas. And each gift we bought—and received—was really from the heart.

I always sought the perfect Christmas and was always disappointed with the gifts and depressed after the holiday. Then this one. Close to perfect.

Day 149, Dec. 25

Another Christmas gone, and I'm dead—as usual. But sober, not as usual. We opened presents when we returned home from 11 p.m. communion. Not a bad present holiday at all. With love.

"When you were dead in your sins, God made you alive with Christ."

Carrie and I went to Dad's grave today. Not an amends, really, but a start. I talked to him about a few things.

Day 150, Dec. 26

Little time to pack, to prepare. We drove straight home, and I went straight to work.

"If the head and the body are to be well, you must begin with the soul; that is the first thing." (Plato)

Day 152, Dec. 28

Getting better about waking and instantly asking God for His will for me today.

Day 153, Dec. 29

I've been having dreams that I slipped. Two nights in a row. And I couldn't remember—in the dream—whether I had. And there was a bridge missing a strand . . .

Who knows what that means? Not I.

Day 154, Dec. 30

A good, lousy, good day. Horrible mistake at the paper. But we recovered. I was down . . . so, I bought a computer. I don't know if it was the right thing to do, but we got a great price. I don't feel as good as I normally do when we buy stuff, and the family was really crabby most of the day. So, we went to the movie. This is the longest I've been without a meeting, and I haven't talked to my sponsor for a week. I don't feel all that good about myself, and I've gained weight. I just need something—time off, time to think, time to pray. Something.

Day 156, Jan. 1, 1996

Work was near perfect. No stress. Just nice. I remember now what I like about it. I had another dream about drinking. It scares me a little.

Meditate: First words in the Bible are about the light God provides. Probably not a coincidence, huh?

Day 157, Jan. 2

I feel better, about myself, about things. But I don't feel good about work. Why? Let's review: I worked twenty-three of thirty-one days in December. I made some mistakes; some things didn't turn out the way I wanted them to. I made assumptions about others' work that turned out to be false. And we made a horrible mistake. I must remember what they told me about feeling good even when the circumstances are bad.

Day 158, Jan. 3

A good day. I'm tired still, but I feel energized. I need to turn my body clock around. I'm working days again. The biggest thing is I made it through a New Year's sober. Mary was never convinced I could or would. I wasn't either. Did anyone notice that they shoot fireworks at midnight? For some reason I had never noticed that before.

CHAPTER 14

High Five

"Therefore confess your sins to each other and pray for each other so that you may be healed."
—James 5: 16

Admitted to God, to ourselves, and to another human being the exact nature of our wrongs.
—Alcoholics Anonymous, step five

It is September, 1971. I am off to college—well, off to junior college in my hometown. Most of the guys I have grown up with, have become close to, are attending another junior college out from Meridian.

I am in a new land, with new people and circumstances.

And I am as uncomfortable as I've ever been. At lunch, instead of going into a cafeteria and trying to find a table at which I could sit by myself (often impossible), or, worse, finding a table at which I would have to sit with someone else, I drive downtown and have lunch at a hamburger joint that makes the best burgers in Meridian.

I am too shy to deal with it all.

✦ ✦ ✦

I eventually overcome the shyness by making myself run for student senate as a sophomore, by joining every service club or organization I can find to join, and by drinking at the inevitable parties that go with the service clubs or organizations. Drinking is the way I compensate for my shyness. It eliminates reservations, both good and bad.

Soon, every time, I'm leading the group. I begin to enjoy leading. I receive praise for my work, for my gifts. My ego grows. My pride in achievement, complimented by men and women, grows.

✦ ✦ ✦

I'm not very shy anymore, although I still find it difficult to say what I really want to say. I fear the rejection that comes with that. After finishing step four to the best of my ability, and getting rid of that draining feeling to some extent, I was forced to look ahead to step five. And fear gripped me.

I was completely okay with telling God everything I had done, confessing, as it were, and asking for his forgiveness. That was no problem. I had done that on nearly an everyday basis for months. But this telling another human being was a different kettle of fear.

I had loads of advice on who should be the recipient of my confession. I was advised that a total stranger might be appropriate. My pastor was suggested, as well.

At first the ideal candidate seemed to be my psychologist. I was already meeting with him on a weekly basis, and in my mind doing much of what was suggested as a plan of attack for step five. I was beginning to listen for the soft whispers of God, however, and the more I prayed about this, the more I listened for God's answer, the more I felt in my heart that this was not the right thing.

I eventually asked my sponsor if he would do it. He said that he would be honored, although it might affect our relationship later. I didn't understand that. What I had done in my life, I thought, was not all that bad. The bodies were deeply buried, still.

✦ ✦ ✦

The Little Red Book says this about step five: "Alcoholic rationalization balks at this honest procedure, discounting the need of admitting anything to another human being. The founders of our movement knew the value of doing this; they knew that only by doing so could we acquire the humility, honesty, and spiritual help necessary to successfully live the AA program."

It's about being honest with ourselves, with God, and with someone else. It's about the humility necessary to admit our greatest faults, our greatest secrets. Just once. Completely. Draining ourselves of all the pride and ego that years have built. Like trees that show their age by the rings they wear, we show our age by the rings of pride that grow.

Honesty and humility. We can't be humble without being totally honest with ourselves. We can't be totally honest with ourselves without a strong sense of humility growing in our souls.

✦ ✦ ✦

It's spring 1963. I'm at the front of my parents' four acres, toward the highway, in the flat part of the property. Daddy plows a quarter acre for spring planting. He calls for me to help. He carefully creates rows, preparing the ground for seeds he'd separated into brown paper sacks. He tells me to dig little holes by hand in the soil, a certain length apart.

As bored as I can be, not listening as usual, sweat popping out on me despite the cool of the early morning, I plop the seeds farther part than he'd like. He yells at me to pay attention.

I yell back, "I don't need to know this stuff. When I get old enough, I'll never do this. I'll have money to pay people to do this for me."

It's spring 1971. We're playing Meridian High School in baseball. We're the country school, the hicks. Meridian is the largest high school in the state. The game is a specially scheduled affair. The Meridian officials had called our high school to schedule the game after both teams had gotten off to great starts. (Meridian would go on to win the state tournament. Every starter in the lineup would either be drafted by major league baseball or sign a grant-in-aid with a college.)

Before the game, Meridian takes batting practice. Their best player, who would be picked in the first round of the free-agent draft later that summer, hits a ball that travels the length of the football field adjacent to the old red-clay infield we are playing on, rolling to a stop in the middle of the infield where we are taking drills.

He trots down from the batting cage slowly. With confident grin on his face, he seeks the ball. He calls to our third baseman, who has retrieved the ball for him, asking if he wants the ball autographed.

Inspired, we win 8-2. It is the only game Meridian loses all season.

✦ ✦ ✦

It's spring, sometime before 30 B.C. Jesus' best friends, the guys he counts on to take his gospel to the world, the guys he knows best, loves most, are talking. Peter, the veteran, crafty pitcher of the team, is talking with John, the catcher, the leader on the field, perhaps the manager's personal favorite. They're arguing about who is most valuable. Can a pitcher, a rock, the guy Jesus will call on when the game's on the line, on the road, against those wily Gentiles, be the most valuable player when he only pitches every four days? Or can the most valuable player only be the guy with the most staying power, the guy who won't die on you no matter how hard the going gets?

They can't settle the argument between themselves, and the

rest of the team is no help either. So they go to Jesus, expecting a vote of confidence.

"Who is the greatest in the kingdom . . ." they ask. They really expect an answer, which perhaps shows their ego more than anything else.

Jesus calls a kid over. He's dirty-faced, hair hanging down in curls, old robe torn and tattered. Jesus says, "I tell you the truth." As if he could tell anything else. It makes him the best of managers. "Unless you change and become like little children, you will never enter the kingdom of heaven.

"Therefore, whoever humbles himself like this child is the greatest in the kingdom of heaven," he says.

They sulk away, wondering how some little leaguer could ever be considered greater than the major league players. Jesus sure talked funny sometimes.

✦ ✦ ✦

Jesus is called a lot of names in the Bible. He's our Lord. He's the prince of peace, the son of man.

But the gospel writers are frightfully short on description of the greatest whoever lived. We know nothing of how tall or short our Lord was. We know nothing of hair color or length. We know nothing of the eyes that could see into the hearts of men. We assume he was dark-skinned. But we know so little of the way he looked. I suspect we wouldn't recognize him if he walked by us today, despite the many paintings on display in our homes, and churches.

But we do have this description of his attitude: "Your attitude should be the same as that of Jesus Christ: Who, being in very nature God, did not consider equality with God something to be grasped, but made himself nothing, taking the very nature of a servant, being made in human likeness. And being found in appearance as a man, he humbled himself." (Philippians 2: 5-8)

He humbled himself.

God, who created the world, who sets those fluffy clouds to drift, who brings us rain, snow, and drought, humbled Himself. He first was born of woman, a thoroughly humbling experience, I'm told. He lived as a poor carpenter's son (again, I relate). He had no formal teaching, no base from which to build a successful life. He was finally jailed, sentenced, and killed as a rebel.

His entire life was built on humility. He had no problems with the boss because of an unhealthy ego run amok.

He never sinned. He was humble. The connection is as obvious as the face we do not see but know in our hearts, with all our hearts.

The Bible says humility, which is the first step in obedience to God, stops quarrels, brings contentment.

✦ ✦ ✦

It is a Friday night in August, 1995, the first Friday I have as a sober adult. Not necessarily the first Friday I've been sober as an adult, but the first time I was fairly confident I wouldn't be drinking.

The treatment center has let me out for the weekend. But Polly, the Nurse Ratched of the ward, says I have to go to an AA meeting. I tell her I'm going to my mother's house for the weekend. She says good. She says I'm also going to an AA meeting. She tells me to use the phone book, find a place to go.

I do. I'm full of pride and ego, but I'm scared spitless of Polly.

I have my mother call for times. It is easier for her, I say. The truth is I'm embarrassed to call.

I go to a 7 p.m. meeting. The club in Meridian is near the park, where, ironically, a ball field used to be. It was where I coached perhaps my greatest little league upset in the first year I coached. The field obviously had been torn down.

I go in. The club is filled. I'm early, but members are milling around, lighting cigarette after cigarette and pouring coffee. They all seem to know each other. I'm back in college, terrified of the strangers. I find a corner couch and sit down, fingering an ashtray nervously.

It's the second AA meeting I've attended, this time around. I'm vaguely aware of the structure of the meeting. I'm also vaguely aware of something called the Holy Spirit. I think nothing much of either as the meeting begins. I listen uninterested as speaker after speaker tells what God has done for them after they made a decision to turn their will over to Him. I wish I were anywhere else. I know who the most valuable player in this building is, and it is me.

Luke 11:14 says, "For everyone who exalts will be humbled." And the Holy Spirit moves me.

I begin to speak. I don't know why. I could have done my penitence, done my time, slipped quietly away from this group, never seen them again, and gone on with my life. Quiet. Not sharing. Not connecting. Not drinking, but not sober.

The Holy Spirit moves me.

I tell my story for the first time at an AA meeting, breaking bits and pieces of my life into a cough-interrupted monologue. I stumble around. I try to address what I see as the problem, even talk a bit about what I see as the solution. I have no clear idea about what I will eventually go through, but I try.

I humble myself, in my own eyes, for the first time. I still tell them what my job, what my career is. I know nothing of true humility at this point. I still measure my worth by what I do for a living, what my status is, what I make, what I own. I still fail to see mistakes made, faults created, false gods worshiped.

But I take the first tiny movement into the huge footprints that He left. He who was above all else made Himself a lowly human, with a humble spirit.

Nothing I've been able to accomplish or that has been accomplished in me came because of what I was able to do. I worked the AA program to the best of my ability. But the inner chance that happened came through the grace of God. God created humility in me through the steps of AA (which obviously are scripturally based). He developed an honest spirit in me.

✦ ✦ ✦

It's fall of 1995. I'm on the golf course. My tee shot, as usual, goes awry. I find the ball under the welcoming upraised roots of a big oak. I pull the ball out from the tree to where I can at least see the green. I hit my second shot low, actually almost clearing the low-hanging tree limbs. I hit my third shot right, pop a wedge short of the green, chip to within twenty feet of the hole, and putt twice, finally sinking a five-footer somehow. I write a "5" on my card. My playing partner has parred the hole, so I'm not putting myself ahead of him. I'm just cheating so I won't shoot too high a score.

Character, I've read, is what you do when no one is watching.

✦ ✦ ✦

As I worked deeper and deeper into my spiritual development, as God began to work through my veins like life-giving substance, it became harder and harder to write that 5 when I shot a 6.

No one knew I was cheating. Just as no one knew I was drinking every night. Just as no one knew I took two dollars out of the cash register on occasion at Post Office Drug when I worked there as a sophomore in college.

No one knew that I never actually played baseball for my junior college, as I claimed I did. No one knew I never graduated from college, because my resume for years said I did. No one knew the deep secrets I kept. No one knew I wasn't the perfect guy I thought I was appearing to be.

Yes, they did. I, through my lack of humility, simply thought they didn't.

As I blew up like a balloon, the fat going to my stomach and my chest, I convinced myself that I looked, acted and felt like I always had. As I grew more tired because of the alcohol I was consuming, I convinced myself that I could still perform as I always had at work, at home and at play, when the facts showed that my performance was tailing off at work and my family was in the beginning stages of exhaustion and disintegration.

My lack of honesty and humility had a stranglehold on my mind and my heart. I couldn't see the effect my drinking, my way of living, my lack of God, was having on everyone I came in contact with.

And the only way out of this was to find honesty and humility. Step five and I had to come face to face

That stranger in the mirror had to begin to speak to me, to God and to another human being.

✦ ✦ ✦

It is December 20, 1995. I arrive early at Shoney's. My sponsor comes five or ten minutes later. We enter, ask for a booth and a pot of coffee. The place is filled.

Behind my sponsor, a man sits, eating baby-back ribs with gusto. To our right, over a small partition, an elderly couple have finished their meal and are puffing on Marlboros and sipping from white coffee cups.

To our left along the wall, tables are full of kids, parents, relatives, all there to enjoy a holiday season meal. They're laughing, talking, listening. Just enjoying themselves. As nearly as I can tell, no one but me is here to bare his soul to another.

I knock back cup after cup of coffee as my sponsor and I exchange small talk. We're not here to talk about our families, but we do. We're not here to talk about work, but we do.

I'm terrified. It's one thing to tell this guy what I've done wrong in my life, down to the barest, darkest detail. It's quite another to tell all of Shoney's. I want a clear, quiet forum for this. I keep the small talk going until people begin to clear out. Finally, I say something like, "I guess we'd better get on with what we're here for."

My sponsor smiles gently, reassures me this won't hurt (much).

And I begin.

I confess all I can think of. As I confess, more than I've even written down comes to mind. I tell that, too. I tell things I won't repeat in this book. I tell things that might not have even been wrong or bad, but I take no chances. I stay completely serious. The part of me that tries to use humor in difficult situations is stone-cold silent. I go through all my relations. I tell about my first marriage. I tell about my fears, my shame. I tell about my father, my mother, my current marriage.

I open the bottle and pour, and the tap stays open for some length of time, almost two hours. I read some of my confession. I tell even more.

I let it go.

On occasion, my sponsor interrupts with advice or confirmation of feeling or a story about something he'd done, trying to show me that what I had done wasn't as strange or bad as I thought. He helps me to understand that there is no reason to hold secrets anymore.

Finally, with all my sins, my wrongs, my indiscretions lifted from me, given to God, I finish. I am tired. Full of caffeine, but tired.

My sponsor tells me to go somewhere, take an hour, think about the first five steps of the program. He tells me to review all I've done in the past five months, make sure I've been thorough. Then come back, meet him at Denny's.

I go home, burn my fourth step in a roaring fire as he's told me to do, kiss Mary, and head off. At first, I can't think of a quiet place to go. Then it hits me. A perfect place. I go to the parking lot of the community ball park. I sit there, a full moon throwing its glory over the lot, alone.

Quiet overcomes me. I hear things, but I don't feel anything, as everyone who has taken the fifth step has told me I would. "You'll feel such a feeling of peace, of relief, of joy, you won't believe it," they've said. I feel nothing except tired. Have I done it wrong? Fear gnaws at me. I hear noises—cars driving by with stereos blaring, a door slamming in the distance, voices in backyards. Anything that can distract me does.

Finally, certain that I'm doing this all wrong, I begin to repeat what little I had committed to memory in church: I believe in God the Father Almighty, maker of heaven and earth; I believe in Jesus Christ, born of . . .

I repeat the Apostle's Creed over, and over, and over, and over, and over. I repeat it until, finally, good God, I see it, I feel it. I know what they mean. I don't feel the guilt; I don't feel the shame. I don't feel the resentment, the anger, the hate. I feel the peace.

It is clear as the cloudless night, as bright as the stars twinkling above: I know I am doing this right.

The hour passes without my realizing it.

I race back to Denny's, arriving a little after my sponsor. I walk into the restaurant, see him sitting at a booth. For once, I want no more coffee. He asks me if I am ready. I say, "Ready for what?" He says, "Ready for step six." I say sure. He says, "You just did it." I smile. I'm lost. He says to follow me. We go into the parking lot. He tells me to kneel.

I say, "Here?"

He kneels.

I follow, knowing more about humility than I've ever dreamed possible. I'm in the parking lot of Denny's, kneeling for prayer. I close my eyes so tightly they hurt. I take the ostrich approach. If I can't see the people staring at me, they can't see me.

He reads from *The Big Book*, the seventh-step prayer: "My creator, I am now willing that you should have all of me, good and bad. I pray that you now remove from me every single defect of character which stands in the way of usefulness to you and my fellows. Grant me strength, as I go out from here, to do your bidding. Amen."

He looks up at me, says I've just finished step seven.

✦ ✦ ✦

I don't think I can completely convey how I felt that night, but I believe it to be close to the feeling I had in the sawdust of the camp meeting when I was eight, close in spirit to the feeling I had in the hospital garage, related in spirit to the night at the AA meeting when I discovered surrender.

All steps. Not written in *The Big Book* or even in the gospel. Steps written on my heart. All part of the journey. Honesty and humility.

They're the utensils God uses. After we're given them, we're able to eat the banquet at the Lord's table. "When I consider your heavens, the work of your fingers, the moon and the stars, which you have set in place, what is man that you are mindful of him, the son of man that you care for him?" (Psalms 8: 3-4)

CHAPTER 15

Journal 7
January 4-February 1

Day 159, Jan. 4

Four great truths of Buddhism: 1) suffering is a fact of life; 2) suffering is caused by attachment; 3) liberation from suffering and reinstitution of human freedom can happen only through detachment; 4) human effort toward detachment must involve all aspects of one's life in a deeply spiritual way.

I can't argue with any of that except they need a dose of Jesus' love in there somewhere.

Day 160, Jan. 5

Joel, my stepfather, is near death. Mom seems okay with it. God has kept him from pain, praise his name. I wish I didn't view it as an opportunity. I trust God forgives my humanity. Someday Jesus will make me a good person, I know.

Day 161, Jan. 6

Mom gave us $1,600. I lead with that instead of the funeral because I'm selfish. Through all the effort man can make, it isn't enough without Jesus. I get better, more healthy, more moral through little steps.

Day 163, Jan. 8
I'm dead tired. I have to watch it. Rest is so vitally important.

Day 164, Jan. 9
Tired. Late. "Those who hope in the Lord will renew their strength. They will soar on wings like Eagles; they will run and not grow weary." (Isaiah 40: 31)

Day 167, Jan. 12
Much cleaning to do. Little time to do it. God will help me, give me strength. Mom called, wanted to come down for a week, but I told her to wait until next weekend. I pray I didn't hurt her feelings.

Some methods for using prayer in a crisis: 1) sharpen your mind by reading St. Paul; 2) memorize, then read again verses about faith; 3) relax, affirm God's presence; 4) pray that the decisions will be the right ones; 5) visualize a good outcome of the crisis.

Remember: "Who is wise and understanding among you? Let him show it by his good life." (James 3: 13)

Day 168, Jan. 13
Harry said this at a meeting: "If God is on my side, who cares who is against me."

Man, if I could just remember that sometimes. It's not what people, anyone, thinks about us, but what God sees or feels or thinks.

That would go a long way toward relieving the stupid insecurity that flows in me, wouldn't it?

Why must we spend so much money to clean the house to the state Mom would be happy with? Why can't we just be ourselves? Why can't, oh, what's the use?

Day 169, Jan. 14
We join the church this morning. Five and a half months after

first going. I've reconciled all my thoughts and feelings about AA and church at this point. Shanna and Carrie won't be there, and that's unfortunate. Shanna is sick and Carrie is staying home.

"That we henceforth be no more children, tossed to and fro, and carried about with every wind of doctrine by the sleight of men." (Ephesians 5: 14)

Day 178, Jan. 23

"The work of the Lord is this . . . to believe in the one He has sent." (John 6: 29)

Sometimes I make this harder than it really is. I don't have to understand any of this to believe it. I don't understand how water exists as ice, but I know it does. If I work on my growth, on my spiritual self, if I let God clean me out, life will grow. I've seen it in many people at the meetings.

A weird day. I did a good job of relieving my boss of some anxiety about work difficulties at lunch. I was honest, loving, helpful. Then I came home and was crappy with the family. I don't understand, really, why that would happen.

"It does not, therefore, depend on man's desire or effort, but on God's mercy." (Romans 9: 16)

Day 179, Jan. 24

This is a faith you can count on. Bad news at work didn't depress me. I'm amazed at the changes in my soul, in my emotions.

"Therefore, do not lose heart."

Day 180, Jan. 25

It helps us to stay positive, no matter the circumstances, if we take the time to stop, look at the good in our lives. And be thankful. You sometimes have to force this, but the benefits are heavenly.

1) We have money for a maid.
2) We are paying our bills as best we can—on time, thank God.

3) Health is abundant.

4) We truly have each other; our attention; our love.

Do I want to keep doing this work? Sometimes I feel God is leading me in a different direction. I don't know. If I get unhappy in what I do, it affects my peace. I must leave if that happens. If God wants me to, I'm gone. My work, however, is not my life. It isn't my wife, my kids, my friends. It isn't my God, as it once was. So why spend a second worrying about it?

Day 182, Jan. 27

For I, Billy Turner, am a holy person to the Lord my God. The Lord my God has chosen me out of all the persons on the face of the earth to be His person, His treasured possession.

This is a revised version. Deuteronomy 7: 6.

It's difficult sometimes to find the self-worth that God sees in the worst of us. Mom sits in judgment on all our actions. In my powerlessness, I take it. My Bible says to honor my mother and father. And I love her so much. But this is hard.

I must remember, must strive to remember, that I am automatically loved by God, so to seek praise from others is a waste of the little time I have on earth.

I am God's valuable possession. To value myself is to praise God's efforts. My weight, my sobriety, my patience, my wisdom, my love—all are products of God's grace and mercy to me. I am completely powerless over people, places, and things. God is power, and God is love. Me—I'm a helpless sinner thankfully washed in the blood of Christ.

Today was difficult. A confrontation with Mom about cleaning. At 5 a.m. she was slamming cabinets, cleaning what was already clean. God bless her. I accept that I can't change her; she is who she is. I try not to judge her. But, she's a Christian the same as I. Where is the reciprocal lack of judgment?

Day 184, Jan. 29

Six months ago I drank rum for no reason at all. My, how

things have changed . . . because those who are led by the Spirit of God are sons of God. Mama is driving me nuts. That's okay. It's not the first time I've been nuts, now is it?

Day 186, Jan. 31
I really thought that when you corrected yourself, when you accepted Christ, tried to live a good, moral life (when the drinks dried up and the salvation began), things would go well. I didn't understand that sometimes that's when the suffering begins.

I understand somewhere inside that if Mom won't accept the kids, my wife, or me for what we are—sinners under repair— then that's her problem, not ours. But I just haven't traveled on the spiritual circuit long enough to make it take over my being. I want to scream; I want to shout; I want to take what I learned from Dad, the element of the family argument, and let her have it.

"God is just; He will pay back trouble to those who trouble you and give relief to you who are troubled and to us as well." (2 Thessalonians 1: 6-7)

The good news, I guess, is that the house could be featured in *Better Homes and Gardens*. Heck, if we had a garden it probably wouldn't have any dirt in it. Mama would have cleaned it.

The Holy Spirit, identified as the comforter in the King James translation, is what kept me going this week. I've felt somewhat in a spiritual plane, waiting for God to lead me to the next obstacle or the next job or the next something.

But the grace of Lord Jesus Christ, the love of God, and the communion with the Holy Spirit combined to keep me going. I'll be honest, my mother's visit was taxing on us all. The kids eventually ran like frightened rats to their rooms for safety. They probably suspected they were about to be sprayed with Lysol.

It wore me out spiritually and Mary physically and made me wonder how two people could differ so much in how they interpret the Bible. But through the Holy Spirit, we have access to the Father. And as I understand it, this minute, this hour, I have a heavenly Father who loves me, and I can do nothing to lose His approval. His Spirit lives in me and He gives me unconditional love. That—and the knowledge that Thursday's Bible group would come eventually—was important to me through a week of constant criticism. Mama says she can't change who she is. I say God can change anyone. I say I'm proof of that. So truly, I am full of power by the Spirit of the Lord. I breathe it in and it refreshes me on a daily basis. Without His spirit, I'm not sure what life would be anymore. I'm not always sure what it is; but I know it's better than it's ever been. And I'm truly grateful. Which might be the biggest change in me of all.

CHAPTER 16

The Fundamentals

May they be brought to complete unity to let the world know that you sent me and have loved them as you have loved me.
—John 17: 23

We are three, you are three, have mercy on us.
—Max Lucado

It is 1965. A typical Sunday morning at the Lockhart Church of God Holiness. I have invited a friend to church. I did not tell him how to dress.

He and his family arrive on time, wearing clean, polished shoes, their hair fixed, the mother wearing rouge and lipstick.

I watch him in the pew next to me. I wiggle forward on the bench and reach back to pull at my underwear. (Church services always have a way of making restless children's underwear bunch up.) The wooden bench, stiff and hard-backed, seems to grow more and more attached to my behind as the preacher's message stretches on toward forty-five minutes.

I have my mind on temporal matters instead of eternal ones. Fried chicken awaits. We're having a potluck lunch after the service, which is the reason I asked my friend and his family to church in the first place. How he got his whole family to come, I don't know. I could never talk Daddy into coming.

The dark-haired preacher with the rosy, crinkled cheeks gathers all the energy left in his body and roars some more. He lifts the black, dog-eared King James translation and slams it to the podium, making thoughts of fried chicken and macaroni and cheese disappear from my mind.

"And when he had taken the book, the four beasts and four and twenty elders fell down before the Lamb, having every one of them harps and golden vials full of odours, which are the prayer of saints," he reads.

"John saw in his revelation, brothers and sisters. Saw. Saw the future. Saw the sinful present. Do you? Do you now ? Bless us, Lord, show us. Do you taste the sweat and feel the suffering of Christians? Do you toil for the Lord? Are you washed clean or are you a sinner ?

"Our time is at hand. Jesus is at hand. Jesus is coming, coming for you, coming for me, as the hymn says. But are you ready? Have you done the work, scraped the heart of misery, prayed the prayers, fallen down before the Lamb and asked his forgiveness?

"Are yours the works of the Lord or of the Devil?"

The preacher's voice rises to a crescendo, scaring half the life out of me.

Members of the congregation, twenty-five or so people from the area who grew up in the church and have never attended another, hang on every word. Murmurs of "Yes, Lord, do it, Lord," float as whispers below the preacher's piercing shouts, flowing with the rhythm of the man's speaking. He hammers, he shouts, he gestures, pointing, pulling the congregation with him.

Sweat, Christian or not, beads on me. The fan droning at the back window of the church is doing little good.

My friend and his family are stunned. My friend's red-and-blue-checked, short-sleeve shirt stands out in a sea of stiff, white long sleeves. No ties. Our church doesn't believe in ties. It's scriptural, I'm told.

I sense Mama about to slide forward off the bench although I haven't really heard the preacher call for prayer. As I pivot, fall to my knees, and begin to rest my head on my hands on the bench, I look over at my friend. He realizes that they are different, knows his family isn't fitting in here. They are actually standing. Of course, they quickly realize their mistake, but my friend's glowing cheeks reveal his embarrassment.

I giggle. Mama shoots a warning glance at me. There's no laughing or playing in church.

✦ ✦ ✦

As I approached six months of being sober, I began to have somewhat independent thoughts about my spiritual journey. I still was going to AA meetings, but certainly not with the frequency of the first three months.

A Bible study group replaced an AA meeting on Thursday, and church replaced an AA meeting on Sunday mornings.

I began to look deeply into the AA program, not just at the steps, but at the background, the history behind the program. If I had God on my side, I began to wonder why I needed AA. The best place to worship God seemed to be in church. Why couldn't the two coexist?

I had shared some of my story at the Bible group, and not only did it not seem to make the people there look down on me, it seemed to help bring the group together. We shared our feelings about Christ with total honesty. We told our doubts, our dreams, our feelings.

Just like at an AA meeting. But, unlike an AA meeting, we were free to worship, to glorify the only savior the world has known. So, I was a little confused.

I felt free to examine where the road was taking me. With only one roadblock in sight.

I, like many AA members, had been shaken and frustrated by our parents' religion. We associated lack of understanding, lack of compassion, and lack of acceptance with the Christian upbringing we'd had. Experiences in our childhoods had stained our faith.

In Phillip Yancey's book composed of columns he wrote for *Christianity Today*, there's one about the Midnight Church. He writes about an alcoholic friend who struggled with a return to church: I asked him to name the one quality missing in the local church that AA had somehow provided. He stared at his cup of coffee for a long time before he said softly this one word: dependency.

No one of us can make it on our own—isn't that why Jesus came? Yet most church people give off a self-satisfied air of piety or superiority. I don't sense them consciously leaning on God or each other. Their lives appear to be in order. An alcoholic who goes to church feels inferior and incomplete. It's a funny thing. What I hate most about myself, my alcoholism, was the one thing God used to bring me back to Him. Maybe that's the redeeming value of alcoholics. Maybe God is calling us alcoholics to teach the saints what it means to be dependent on Him and on His community on earth.

I can't argue that there was more acceptance at the AA meetings than I have felt many times when I've been in church. More friendliness. More instant understanding that we were tied together in a fight for life. Perhaps the most important factor was that often at AA meetings, there was the absolute blessed admittance that we were broken and could find no other help. Sometimes in church I've felt that we believe we're fixed or that we need to fix others.

Some of that feeling, that judgmental attitude comes into me because of how I thought all churches and all church people were supposed to be. I had what is now known as a fundamentalist upbringing. There were many don'ts in the Bible as we were taught it; I can't remember many dos.

Yancey provides a test that can indicate whether someone had a fundamentalist upbringing, as I did:

1) Do you have trouble getting close to people?
2) Do you believe God is capricious?
3) Do you believe your body is ugly?
4) Do you believe the world is a bad place?
5) Do you have difficulty having fun?
6) Are you quick to judge others?
7) Do you tend to think in either/or, black/white?
8) Do you believe sex is bad?
9) Are you afraid you are going to hell?

I would add, do you think you can work your way into heaven? Do you believe that you have no hope? Are you wracked with guilt over what you do, even if you don't want to do it?

Did your church suppress emotions, tell you anger is bad, tell you, you are bad? Did your church tell you fun is bad? Did your church teach you that joy and happiness lead to pride, which is a sin? Yet, did your church have a yearly revival at a campground where emotions were the key to salvation? If you weren't able to cry for Jesus, was your faith weak?

Did your church teach you about the grace of God?

If mine did, I don't remember it. I learned that I had every chance of going to hell because the devil was powerful. I learned nothing of the power of Jesus to change lives. I learned that Jesus would save us, but I didn't learn he could heal us. Heal us of what? Of being legalists who squeeze out the very love of life.

✦ ✦ ✦

How does God lead? With me, I believe he led me to books, to people, to places that would give me help if I would accept it.

In October, I went to a giant book sale at a seminary in the area. I'd never bought a book on spirituality in my life, my tastes then running toward Stephen King and Dean Koontz.

But there in that little room I picked up two books, *Of the Imitation of Christ* by Thomas Kempis and *Joy All the Way* by Stanley Collins.

The book on joy, written in 1976, told me about a joyless life being a burdensome life. It told me that joy is never an end in itself, that the search for joy is like searching for a pot of gold at the end of the rainbow. But—and this was perhaps most important then in my search—joy is the by-product of "a right relationship with God, the fruit of living in close fellowship with Him, the outcome of a daily obedience to Him."

It made sense to me. And peace is the by-product of His love.

Then I read Kempis' book, written in the 1400s. Later I would learn that John Wesley had read it. (Wesley founded the Methodist Church, of which I am a member.)

Kempis was a monk in a Netherlands monastery when he wrote the book. He "walked with Christ in such intimacy" that the book is a rich inheritance to millions of Christians. His main point, among many others, was that we should not only persist through tribulations, but should welcome them. We should imitate not only the life of Christ, but should also accept and imitate the suffering.

That did not give me joy. I couldn't understand nor do what this book wanted me to, and I soon put it down.

"Many He has who are desirous of consolation, but few of tribulation," Kempis wrote. "Many He finds who share His table, but few His fasting. All desire to rejoice with Him, few are willing to endure anything for Him."

I believe God led me to this book so that I would know that this search isn't just healing and happiness.

I spoke to my psychologist soon after about this subject. It was a difficult concept to embrace. He asked me what I was searching so hard for. I told him happiness. "I want a life where

I can be happy. That's all. Just happy."

"Would you settle for peace?" he asked.

I pondered what he said. My first reaction was to say no. I wanted to be happy. I told him I would think it over.

And the search continued.

At a gospel bookstore, I found a book by Charles Swindoll, whom I had never heard of, written in 1990, called *The Grace Awakening*. It was another step in the changing of my mind and body. This book helped take away what my mother would again put on me. Jesus' yoke is an easy one if we let it be. Mother's was hard.

Swindoll says that grace is the opposite of a doctrine called humanism, the theory that through their work, and talent, human beings can save themselves. (I am the master of my fate. I run the show. I direct the play.)

With grace, which is a free gift of salvation, God does the saving. God is the master of my fate. He runs the show. He hires the actors. My part? I accept the lead role, or decline it if I so choose.

Further, grace is not (as some churches would have you believe) a way to impose more laws, restrictions, joy killers on Christians than could ever be found in the Bible. It does not break the moral law found in the Old Testament. It fulfills it, in the presence of Christ.

I read a portion of Swindoll's book that set me to thinking.

> *Accepting others is a basic to letting them be. How about those in our life who may disagree with us on issues that are taboos in evangelical Christian circles today? Here are a few: going to the movies or live theater; wearing cosmetics; playing cards; watching television; going to the beach; not having a quiet time every morning or at least every day; going to a restaurant that sells liquor; wearing certain clothing; wearing certain clothes; driving certain cars; wearing certain jewelry; listening to certain*

music; dancing; holding a certain job; wearing your hair a certain way; having lovely and elegant possessions; getting a face lift; drinking coffee; eating certain foods; working out in leotards.

I would add drunks who smoke, or homosexuals who are repentant, or black men and women who love the Lord with all their being.

Or young kids with checkered shirts or pasts.

We're all going to the same place, but we choose so many different ways to get there. If only we could just accept that we are loved by the same God, who loved us so much that He took the form of a human to die for us.

C.S. Lewis, probably the most renowned Christian writer other than Paul, wrote in 1929, "When all is said (and truly said) about divisions of Christendom, there remains, by God's mercy, an enormous common ground."

I believe this. And, as the winter grew long, I began to try to merge the two major forces in my life. I tried to explain to Mama that you can smile in church. As simple a statement as that. You can worship with joy. I accept that there will be bad times in the future, times where the lesson to be learned is a harsh one. I accept that God is working in me to produce a Christ-like perfection that He will take into His home at some future moment. I accept that I will fail at times, even though I try to do God's will.

And I have blessed, complete assurance that God will forgive me when I do. No works, nothing I do will save me, will keep me dry, will keep me happy.

But God can. That is the sovereign God whom I worship. But I do not worship a God who is hanging around and watching my every move, just waiting for me to mess up so He can go "aha" and pounce. He forgives me my sins, all of them. From that gratitude comes my obedience. From that love comes the effort to do the right thing, to take the long day's journey into right. Not from blind, stupid obedience but from all-seeing, knowledgeable obedience that comes from love.

I love Jesus for what he did and for what he's doing.

So, a mixture of AA and Methodism began to emerge. I was Scrappy, the dog of spiritualism, a blend, a mixture.

I had friends, people I believed in on either side of the line. There were AA people who wouldn't see the inside of any church, sometimes out of anger at what they perceived as less-than-accepting glances from members, sometimes out of shame. I had church friends who accepted me, but I wasn't sure what they would make of Harry, or John, or Steve.

I belonged to a program that allowed me to be a member simply by saying I wanted to quit drinking. It claimed a spiritual, not a religious base. I had the hardest time separating the two words.

Then I read a story by Max Lucado.

A bishop was traveling by ship to visit a church across the ocean. While en route, the ship stopped at an island for a day. He went for a walk on a beach. He came upon three fishermen mending their nets.

Curious about their trade, he asked them some questions. Curious about his ecclesiastical robes, they asked him some questions. When they found out he was a Christian leader, they got excited. "We Christians!" they said, proudly pointing to one another.

The bishop was impressed but cautious. Did they know the Lord's Prayer? They had never heard of it.

"What do you say, then, when you pray?"

"We pray, 'We are three, you are three, have mercy on us.'"

The bishop was appalled at the primitive nature of the prayer. "That will not do." So he spent the day teaching them the Lord's Prayer. The fishermen were poor but willing learners. And before the bishop sailed away the next day, they could recite the prayer with no mistakes.

The bishop was proud.

On the return trip, the bishop's ship drew near the island again. When the island came into view, the bishop came to the deck and recalled with pleasure the men he had taught and resolved to go see them again. As he was thinking a light appeared on the horizon near the island. It seemed to be getting nearer. As the bishop gazed in wonder, he realized the three fishermen were walking toward him on the water. Soon all the passengers and crew were on the deck to see the sight.

When they were within speaking distance, the fishermen cried out, "Bishop, we come hurry to meet you."

"What is it you want?" asked the stunned bishop.

"We are so sorry. We forget lovely prayer. We say, 'Our Father, who are in heaven, hallowed be your name,' and then we forget. Please tell us prayer again."

The bishop was humbled. "Go back to your homes, my friends, and when you pray say, "We are three, you are three, have mercy on us."

He said there would be one body. And I believe that in the many-roomed mansion the Father calls home, there are enough rooms for every hurting individual on this hurting planet. It's not the tradition of either the church or AA that saves us. It's not the rituals. It's not in the faces, the minds, or the words. It's in the hearts or it's not.

It isn't enough to sob when you mention the name of Jesus, then complain that black people are the reason the world is in the shape it's in. It isn't enough to abhor homosexuality while ignoring the compassion Jesus would have had for the sinner. It isn't enough to take communion on Sunday and take pride in your accomplishments on Wednesday. It isn't enough to acknowledge your sins only with the complete assurance that they aren't as bad as the next person's, thereby lifting yourself above others.

Swindoll, whom I believe to be a real man of God in the

best sense of the phrase, wrote in his book *Dropping Your Guard* that the "whip routine" of Christianity has to go. A few of those whips include: "Attempting to pressure people to 'straighten up' before they're able to get on their feet; forcing people to become more and more like we are; expecting adherence to highly structured demands, tight-fisted rules and rigid requirements; placing the painful twist of legalistic demands; forcing others to give up certain habits and adapt to our set of preferences."

The most important thing to understand about alcoholics is that they are us. They are just like us. There is no greater or lesser sin. I have a genetic disposition toward alcohol; thus my alcoholism is the tip of the iceberg, a portion of my sin. My denial, my pride, my ego, my separation from God are all part of that iceberg. But Jesus is the cleanser of them all.

Alcoholics who reject "religion" are not rejecting Christ, necessarily. They are rejecting rejection. They are rejecting the feeling that they're not wanted at "our" church.

Just who is supposed to be in the church, I ask?

It's for the hurting, the miserable, the malcontents, the damaged, the sick, the dying. Jesus came to save sinners. Alcoholics Anonymous does save sinners from alcohol, but we owe it to all alcoholics to give them more. Their, our, twelve steps are but the bridge to the thirteenth step, to Jesus. If the church isn't a place where I can cry, where I can be honest, where I can seek God, what is it?

Jesus says the only way to the Father is through Him. Bill Wilson never acknowledged that in his program. So that is the problem I have with AA. Many churches never acknowledge that Jesus heals as well as saves.

I'm living, breathing, thinking, thanking, loving proof of that.

I truly began to understand that through a bit of Bible study.

PART THREE

Deeper and Deeper

CHAPTER 17

Journal 8
February 2-29

Day 189, Feb. 3

A difficult day. Very difficult. The van is near death. It was the starter this time. I must pray for what to do next. Do we get something else with the income tax check, or do we repair this thing? I was horrible today. I yelled at everyone.

Day 190, Feb. 4

Bitterly cold, but I feel okay. Physically my stomach troubles me. Spiritually, I'm okay. Although I didn't attend a meeting. I'm concerned about how difficult it is for me to spend good quality time with the kids.

Day 191, Feb. 5

"The people walking in darkness have seen a great light." (Isaiah 9: 2)

I have a half pack of cigarettes. Truly I must quit. Whatever comes between God and me must be done away with.

However, in Romans 9:16 it clearly says, "It does not, therefore, depend on man's desire or effort, but on God's mercy."

"God will . . . have mercy on whom . . . he has mercy." (Exodus 9: 16)

I can't quit without Him. I admit I am powerless over nicotine and my life is unmanageable in regard to smoking. I need God's help.

10:30 p.m. I still haven't quit. I folded. It is such a fine, fine line between being self-confident and full of ego. If the self-confidence grows from God, it is pure and good. If the ego is of the flesh and the world and is boastful, it is bad, I believe.

Self-examination: Where does my confidence come from?

Day 193, Feb. 7

Yesterday was great for most of the day. I was full of grace, totally at peace and full of joy. But I went to a Methodist men's meeting and felt some of that suck out of me. They spent a lot of time arguing about the cost of eggs for a breakfast held last week. It had nothing to do with God as far as I could tell. This wasn't for me at this time. Carrie's grades were shown to me. For the second straight week, they were bad. We need some work there. But what God has done for me is let me accept the down times for what they are. We lost a foot of water out of the pool, also.

When the bad times come, as they will, for the first time I have a rock. I have someone to talk to about them. Someone who will listen. Someone who has the power to help.

Day 194, Feb. 8

"My son, if you accept my words, and store up my commands within you, turning your ear to wisdom and applying your heart to understandings . . . then you will understand the fear of the Lord and find the knowledge of God." (Proverbs 2: 1-5)

Bible study:

To me this speaks about God's great plans for us. He allows us to make our mistakes, make our decisions, make our way down those bad turns through job failures, through church attendance falloffs, through every good and bad decision we can make. But we have to be ready to accept the consequences of our decisions. I believe that God causes or allows everything in the world—always for a purpose, we though certainly we may not understand it. Nothing that I can find in the Bible says everything is going to be perfectly good in our lives if we are Christians. It says we will be blessed—and the blessing I want is the peace and joy that lives within me through the Holy Spirit to be with me always, through temptation and through pain, through bad times, through it all. God is faithful. Need we know more?

Day 195, Feb. 9

I was bad today. We went to a Mardi Gras parade, and I stared at the many, many who could drink and apparently stay somewhat normal. I wished for a brief moment that I was one of them. I had a good, patient time, however. Carrie had a spell afterward when she wasn't allowed to bring someone over and eventually she cried, pouted, all the normal things. I took it and took it and I couldn't leave it alone, and finally I erupted. Just like my father would have. I hate it when I do that. So why did I do it?

1) I should know Carrie always acts that way when she's turned down;

2) I shouldn't let her actions affect me in any way, for I was doing the right thing;

3) I should never let a disturbance with Carrie bleed over into a tirade against Mary.

It takes so long for Christ to work in us. I pray for patience. I pray for help. Sometimes I feel it's there. Sometimes I don't.

Day 196, Feb. 10

I can drink. I have that option. No one on earth or in heaven can tell me I can't. It is lawful. It won't even damage me, immediately, to do so. But I know, or have learned, that one drink, just one, just a sip really, because I have a disease that doesn't permit me the choice of stopping, would keep me from the opportunity to reason and to hear God's word. For that reason, I choose not to drink. It is the holy thing to do. I have never been good enough to earn grace, but I don't believe grace will be given until I humble myself by remembering my affliction of alcoholism on a daily basis. Praise be to God that I have this disease.

Day 197, Feb. 11

"Light has come into the world, but men loved darkness instead of light because their deeds were evil." (John 3: 19)

Alice asked me to give the opening prayer at the evangelism commission meeting, so I composed this:

"Dear Lord,

"We thank you and bless your name for allowing us to be here tonight. In Job, the writer said he would lay his cause before you, for you perform wonders that cannot be fathomed, miracles that cannot be counted. We believe in those miracles, both large and small, Lord. Tonight we ask you to guide us to your perfect will, and that is the miracle we call on tonight. Let us understand your will and have the courage and power to carry it out. Thank you for your grace that allows this church to exist. In your son's name we ask these things."

What are the goals in my life?

I need to ask this question more often. God has a plan. I need to follow it. I don't even know if what I do for a living is what God wants me to do.

Day 198, Feb. 12

I can make my life abundant through Christ, but I must not do anything that numbs the consciousness.

Day 199, Feb. 13

Mary met a woman yesterday who said, "Your husband recently found the Lord, didn't he? The Holy Spirit told me last night that I would meet a woman whose husband was doing God's work."

I have no idea what that means. I want to do God's work. But I don't know what that is right now.

Day 200, Feb. 14

Sometimes is seems like it is all too much. People I don't know are talking about us. I promise I haven't said anything or done anything to attract attention. I'm trying to remain humble. But meetings at the church, meetings at AA, work without stopping all get to me. There is never a contemplative moment. And there's the AA problem. Do I need AA? If so, I need to finish step nine. I've done or I do steps ten and eleven on a daily basis and by becoming chairperson of the Monday night group, I'm continuing step twelve. In April, I plan to go to Jackson for a meeting with Suzie, my first wife. I only need three or four people to complete it.

Day 201, Feb. 15

Last night was horrible. Let me count the ways. I left work early to take the family to a good restaurant for a Valentine's dinner. I got home and the backyard had burned. Two kids had been playing with matches outside the yard, and the grass caught on fire. Shanna put it out with the hose. Then, we couldn't find a place to eat. I lost my temper in Luther's because Shanna was pouting about having to eat barbecue. I lost my temper badly in the parking lot of Ryan's, cursing, threatening someone over a parking spot and ripping my best coat. I eventually crashed. I slept twelve hours.

I've got to let go of it. I did it. It happened. I'm sorry. I'm not perfect. In fact, I'm pretty bad. But God loves me. What a deal.

"May all who say to me, Aha, Aha! turn back because of their shame." (Psalm 70: 3)

Day 202, Feb. 16

Bible study:
1:17 "For the law was given through Moses; grace and truth

came through Jesus Christ." (John 1: 17)

This is puzzling for me. It is a continuing theme in recent weeks. If God knew man would have such difficulty with the law, if He knew He would find fault with the people, then why wait all those years for redemption? I believe it is because He knows the nature of His creations and it took those years to let the laws be written on their hearts. No matter what we do, we can never be good enough to gain God's grace. So the new covenant was God's way of saying, "Okay, Billy. You can't help it. To an extent, you're who you are. But I love you, and here is this fresh supply of cleanser. Wash in it, learn a little more about yourself, and you'll be all right. And if you break one of my laws, ask me for forgiveness, believe in my son and you'll be fine. I love you even though I know you're flawed. And I am faithful. You can believe me. I'll always love you."

Day 203, Feb. 16

"The most important thing we can do to stay in the race is to fix our eyes on Jesus." (Hebrews 13: 20)

Last night's Bible study was wonderful. It lifted me, despite the horrible news about Christy, Cathy and Roger's daughter, who might have a tumor. We pray for her. We pray for them. We pray for their comfort.

Day 204, Feb. 19

To be like Jesus means:
1) to accept our roots;
2) to engage the world's pain and struggle;
3) to commit ourselves to other believers.

Day 205, Feb. 20

I must slow down from time to time. "Peace, be still," Jesus told the wind and the waves. I'm not given this gift of sobriety so that I can save the world, at least till I've learned what God wants me to do. If I charged out now, I might mess up someone.

But I won't be a passive Christian. I won't. I want to take what I'm given and give it away. The joy, the Spirit that lives in me when I let him, when I remove self from me by virtue of the Holy Spirit, it's the absolute best, most joyous feeling I've ever had. Even beats the Braves winning the World Series.

Day 206, Feb. 21
God's will: Exactly what I would do if I knew all the facts.
William Temple: "Conversion is to give as much of yourself as you can to as much of God as you can understand, and to do so every day."

Day 209, Feb. 24
What is this search really about? I need to watch myself or the peace I seek, the goodness and the meaning will be for naught. This all must be for the glory of God. Not so people will think more of me. But I walk in confidence, with great self-esteem. While life now and forever has meaning because of the faith I'm given.

What is this search for? There was a guy tonight who'd been in and out of the rooms of AA for ten years. He struggles to keep a job. He got his family back fairly recently, and he slipped a couple of weeks ago. I could see pain in his eyes—the way they focused on the wall instead of the people in the room. He said he knew he had done wrong. He made the decision. But in the deepest part of his heart, he knew he didn't want that drink. How powerless we are. I could be him but for the sweet cleansing grace of Jesus. I'm a devoted Christian, a learning sinner who is a spiritual work-in-progress. But I'm also an alcoholic, a diseased loser who could lose it all—not Jesus' love but the ability to ask for it—with one sip of beer. I can't stop drinking, but with the power of the Holy Spirit, I don't have to drink today. And my sharing of that power, my witness of the mercy of Jesus Christ, is what I can give to AAs everywhere. It keeps me sober.

Day 213, Feb. 28

What points do I want to make at Bible study on Thursday?

1) The Holy Spirit visits us every Thursday; of that I have no doubt. He energizes me. He teaches us; He surely comforts me.

2) I'm a lousy comforter. I struggle to love, to show love, even to feel love. For my friends. For the people who have stretched out their hands to help me.

3) I'm immature spiritually, relationally, emotionally, morally. But the Holy Spirit has taken my hand for reasons I can't know or understand and is leading me places I never imagined I would go.

4) I love everyone in the room with a type of love I never knew existed. It comes from being loved on an unconditional basis by a power I didn't even realize knew I existed.

5) I feel the pain, the worry, but I'm a poor, poor place to go for help.

6) I do however, know where to go for help.

Day 214, Feb. 29

Seven months of sobriety: a lifetime and a moment.

CHAPTER 18

Friendship:
Gains and Losses

Unless I see the nail marks in his hands and put my finger where the nails are, and put my hand into his side, I will not believe it.
—John 20: 25

It is 1958. We live in a two-bedroom house in the projects constructed for GIs returning home from World War II, in a poor section of Meridian.

I'm playing outside the little red-bricked house with my friend, Jaboni. I'm trying to dig a hole that will go to China. Mama said that I could dig a hole that deep, and Jaboni and I are digging it. I'm the only one who can see Jaboni, but I count on his help.

I can always count on Jaboni, my best friend. I talk to him, tell him secrets, tell him when he's good and when he's bad. When I reach a certain age, can no longer see or talk to or hear Jaboni. It's difficult when friends go away, isn't it?

✦ ✦ ✦

It's 1959. Daddy and Mama buy the white house atop the

hill in the little community of Lizelia. It's bigger than the very small one we had in town. And it's in the country, where Mama wants to live. It has acreage and beauty instead of the closeness of the projects.

But to me, all it means is leaving Rickey and Tommy, my best friends. We play together every day. They'd been with me when I took the dare and climbed that one extra limb, only to fall and cut my arm deeply in two places on a chain-link fence.

They showed the true measure of friendship by running all the way to my house to tell Mama what had happened, although in some ways it was their fault for daring me.

Leaving them nearly kills me. How can I ever have friends like these again? How can I start over? It has always been so hard for me to make friends. I'm so shy; talk is difficult for me. I've never had friends like these two brothers.

✦ ✦ ✦

It's 1971, spring. I'm lying on my bed, looking out the window. The wind is being pulled in by the big fan we'd bought at a sale when they'd auctioned off fixtures at the Meridian library. It is cool, and the air is sweet.

I'm a senior in high school. About to graduate. About to leave all I've known since we moved to this house when I was eight. All my friends, Rickey, Stanley, Kenny Joe, Sonny, Randy, are about to be gone. What will I do now?

How do I cope? How do I make new friends? Every one of them is going to East Mississippi Junior College. I'm going to Meridian JC. It's a new world. A new environment.

How can I ever find friends like these again?

✦ ✦ ✦

It's 1991. We're having a tremendous going away party. The newspaper I worked on has sprung for a room in one of the better restaurants in Jackson. Twenty-four guys I've worked with for years are there to say good-bye to me. I've taken a position in New Orleans.

The hardest part of making the decision to leave Jackson was the thought of leaving these guys. I drink heavily, finally being driven to the hotel in which the family is staying by a guy I'd worked with for ten years.

How can I ever find friends like these again?

✦ ✦ ✦

There's a story in the Bible that reflects what I believe is the true meaning of friendship, which is hugely important in this spiritual journey.

It's a Tuesday evening. The sun in Jerusalem is setting. The heat is oppressive. The friends are meeting together in fellowship. Many there are smiling, their parched lips barely able to grin widely enough. Their leader, their mentor, their teacher, their friend has returned. They had thought he was lost to them forever, that they would never see him again.

Thomas is sitting at a rough wooden table, sipping bitter wine from a clay serving dish. He feels bitter himself, eaten inside by loss and fear. Many in the gathering try to cheer him. They tell him of seeing the risen Jesus a day earlier. "He's back," they say, "back to lead us, back to take this country by storm. If death itself can't defeat this man, who can?"

Thomas sneers, stares at the old walls of the two-story flat the believers have taken refuge in.

He recalls the times with Jesus. He'd believed so deeply in him. He'd followed him for three years, doing whatever he was told. True, he often didn't understand the man, understand what he was telling his friends. But that didn't matter. You could look at Jesus and feel courage and strength that you had never felt before.

Thomas recalls the time Jesus stopped the wind and the waves with only a shout.

A lone tear forms at the edge of one of Thomas's brown eyes, and rolls down a rough, bearded cheek. He recalls Lazarus and smiles. "Lazarus, come out," Jesus had yelled. Why, if Jesus hadn't specifically called for Lazarus, Thomas thought, everyone in those tombs might have gotten up and walked out.

Or would they?

Thomas struggles with the thoughts. Jesus had shown such miraculous powers, such Godliness. He had eaten with sinners, mourned with friends. Thomas couldn't remember a time when Jesus had neglected anyone. Surely he was the Christ? Surely.

If so, Thomas thinks, taking a sip of wine, then why am I sitting here without him? Why didn't he just come down from that ugly piece of wood they'd nailed him to? Why am I so alone in the middle of this crowd? Do they all share this dream of him walking?

I waited, he thinks. I waited Friday night. I waited Saturday. I walked, quickly I admit, past that tomb. Where was he? Where was my Lord?

We'd been through so much, Thomas thinks. He coughs, struggles with the thought, sips again at the wine. When he wanted to go to Lazarus and we were fearful for his life, hadn't I said we'd go together. I was willing to die for him. I was willing.

Jesus knew. He knew Thomas had been willing.

So why couldn't it have been Thomas? Why?

The tears roll down, like the tomb in front of that cave.

Peter comes to comfort him, having seen Thomas's mood. Peter and John had seen Jesus, but they'd failed to see how Thomas had been affected by the death.

Peter, huge Peter, the Lord's rock, walks over, places a big hand on Thomas' shoulder and shakes him. "Thomas. Friend. Why are you so sad? We have seen the Lord."

Thomas bolts, shakes the hand from his shoulder, and rages, knocking over the chair he was sitting in.

"Unless I see the nail marks in his hands and put my fingers where the nails were, and put my hand into his side, I will not believe," Thomas roars. He bolts away from Peter and John, leaving the surprised, disappointed brethren in his wake.

For a week he roams the dirty streets of Jerusalem. He's alone in a city full of his countrymen. He doesn't stop by friends' houses to share tales of the Lord. He doesn't speak of what he's seen or felt or learned of the kingdom of God. During the day, when the overpowering heat burns the skins of the Jews of the city, he slips into shadow and mopes. At night, when the temperature dips relentlessly, he finds a fire he can share with those who want no talk, who are just as lonely and despondent as he, for other reasons.

He craves something, some attention, some help, but he refuses to ask. Finally, at the end of the week, he journeys back to the believers, maybe to argue, maybe to mourn with them. Surely they now have reached the understanding he had from the moment that tomb didn't open on Saturday night.

Thomas knocks on the weather-beaten door. Those inside invite him in excitedly, with hugs, pats on the back. They shut the door behind him and lock it.

Time passes. Though Thomas is still unhappy, he does mix better with those who are lively and happy. He figures he must go on with life. What happened has happened.

Suddenly, there is movement to his right. Though the door to the flat is locked, Jesus enters.

Jesus.

Here.

Thomas looks into those eyes, into that face, so gentle but so strong. He can't believe his tired eyes. This can't be. Jesus here.

Jesus walks over slowly, calmly. The believers part, like the Red Sea, to allow him entrance. He walks past a smiling John, past a smirking Peter, past a laughing Andrew, to Thomas, sitting at the table.

"Peace be with you," he says to the gathering, while looking only at Thomas.

"Put your finger here; see my hands. Reach out your hand and put it into my side. Stop doubting and believe," Jesus says to Thomas.

Thomas reaches a shaking, shamed hand toward his friend. He gently fingers the hands, where gnarled tissue—swollen and red but healed—reveals the holes. He pulls his hands, now calmer, stronger, away to the ugly wound in the side.

He looks up into those eyes, the most special eyes through which sight has ever come, and cries out, "My Lord and my God."

He sobs, shaking and shamed about his disbelief.

And Jesus does what he always, always does. He quiets Thomas, hugs him in an embrace strong enough to mountains. He lifts his friend's head, taking his chin and pulling him from the shame into the love of the deity. "Because you have seen me, you have believed. Blessed are those who have not seen and yet have believed," he says to Thomas and the rest of the gathering.

They all descend upon Jesus, the crowd closing in to touch, to hold, to recall. Friends gathered simply to love.

✦ ✦ ✦

It was stressed in treatment that we must change things: our environment, our friends, our family if necessary.

I was lucky, again. I really had no friends to change. I had become so isolated, shut up in my room and away from anything except my family, that it was not a problem.

I had acquaintances, people I saw and was friendly with on a daily basis at work. They were people I cared about, but for all the wrong reasons. This I learned.

But friends? To me friends were people who came over to the house, had coffee, and talked about kids; maybe you watched a movie together, or took walks or played a game of horse on the driveway.

Friends were people you could trust, to whom you would give your secrets and who you would protect and serve with your life if need be. I was remarkably short of such people. Nobody.

There's a tale in Aesop's fables about two men who were traveling through a dark forest. As they were making their way around a turn, a huge bear jumped out at them.

One of the men climbed a tree, obviously thinking of his own safety first. The other, who knew instinctively he could not fight the bear by himself, fell to the ground and played dead. He had heard that a bear would not touch a dead body. The bear walked around him on all fours, sniffing, scuffling, then walked away without touching the man.

The man in the tree climbed down, shivering in fear. He snickered in relief and said, "It almost looked as though the bear whispered something in your ear. What did he say?"

The other man said, "The bear said that it is not wise to keep company with a fellow who would desert his friend in a moment of danger."

At various times in my life I had friends I thought would never desert me. But the most interesting phenomenon kept repeating itself. If I went away, they simply kept on with their lives and forgot me. And with the inability to ingest much alcohol without acting quite stupid, and with the equal inability to keep from ingesting a lot of alcohol once I had drunk any, I went away a lot.

I never questioned why I didn't have real friends, friends who would call me or come over. It took much thought and the healing grace of Jesus to get me to look at myself. Had I been a good friend? Ever? I was more interested in friends than in anything but my immediate family, really. But I was interested in what they could give me, not in what love I could give them.

Loving Jesus, learning from the Holy Spirit, I discovered something vital to my recovery and, I believe, to anyone's.

You can't do it alone. You must have support.

If you are going to quit drinking, stop any sin, you must rely on God for the strength first. But you must also rely on good friends, old or new, to help. That's the meaning of the AA sponsor; it is someone to talk to, someone who has been through what you're going through.

We've discussed humility and honesty as two of the most vital components of recovery. But building, or rebuilding, trust is important also. You must look deep and see the trusts you've betrayed as you broke promise after promise. Perhaps you, like me, lost the ability to trust in others after they have hurt you or left you or just weren't there for you.

This takes time, effort and grace. The grace God supplies is not only for forgiveness; it's also for rebuilding trust. It starts with the ability to trust in a faithful God. A forgiving God you've perhaps felt already. But you must equally understand that God is faithful. What He promises, He delivers.

If you understand and believe, it becomes easier to accept the idea that people can be faithful as well. You cannot put all your faith in them, in any human, for they are fallible. But there are people you can trust. I know because God put some of them in my life. And He lets me understand that I need only love them, not worry about what they think of me. It is vitally important to my recovery.

When you don't expect anything in return, you can give to

others simply because it is a good thing to do.

It was Thomas' expectations that clouded his belief. He expected one thing of Christ and got another. He had seen miraculous things and expected them to be ushering in the reign of a king. He never understood until Jesus was dead that the kingdom wasn't what Thomas had imagined. He was absolutely crushed when Christ was crucified. That Friday afternoon when his Lord, his friend, had died was the worst moment of Thomas's life.

How many times I've been hurt by friends. They didn't do anything wrong. They simply didn't meet my expectations. I failed to understand that what those expectations were was more my problem than theirs.

I knew from the beginning of my spiritual journey that I wanted to do something about the absolute loneliness I felt. It had nothing to do with the family, with my feelings about them, but with what I felt I needed so that I could be a complete, loving, good person. I didn't want to leave this world without someone somewhere caring. I remembered that funeral home full of Daddy's admirers and wondered what my own funeral would be like.

I had decided to hold a pity party and make myself the main celebrant. As winter came to an end, I was making a dent in the problem, I felt. I knew many people in AA. You can't help but become acquainted with people when you go to almost ninety meetings in ninety days.

Not one of them had invited me to fellowship in the back room over a game of pool. I didn't know what to make of that. I didn't let it bother me. But I did notice.

God took care of my situation, however. I believe he puts people in our lives who are good for us. And I believe the Holy Spirit cared nothing about my playing pool.

Instead, he had Cathy, Roger, Kalynn, Dorsey, and Sherri—a Bible study group of seekers—in mind for me. The lessons I learned about friendship, caring, suffering, life, the possibility of death, and how to deal with loss were as valuable to my growth as any.

✦ ✦ ✦

How does God work in our lives, place his hand on circumstances, bring about those coincidences that shape our experiences?

Mary and I join a Sunday school class because we meet Kalynn in the hallway the first morning we go to the church. We go to this church because we'd tried another one. We call ahead to find out what time church begins. We arrive as the members are leaving the church. They'd changed the time of the morning service, but somehow hadn't told the secretary.

God's move number one. He doesn't want us at the other church.

We walk through the hallway, trying to find someone we can ask about what class we should attend. One person suggests one thing, someone else another. Finally Kalynn appears and we are handed off to her.

Her arms are filled. She is in a rush. She is scrambling to make it to her class on time, dropping pamphlets and papers here and there. She has a pencil stuck behind her ear, pushing back her soft, black hair. She smiles at the two of us, tells us to follow her. She takes us to her class, although supposedly there are age restrictions and such. Her smile is warm, inviting. She proves to be the most enthusiastic person in Christ I will meet. She rolls in the Spirit, soaking it in, giving it away. She's charming, funny, sincere, loving. At thirty-three, she has three children, with a fourth to come before the year is out. She is a person we all should meet. God puts her in our lives to show us how to praise Him.

God's move number two. No Kalynn, no Sunday school class. No Sunday school class, no Bible study. No Bible study— I refuse to think about that.

Two months pass. We're sitting in the class. Kalynn mentions a Bible study that is beginning. Mary and I express interest. I need it; Mary wants it. We go.

We go to the first group two weeks later. Seated there are Dorsey and Sherri, the newest members of the church, a couple who are a decade or more younger than Mary and I. Dorsey is a psychologist by trade whose love is marathon running; he is short with a runner's build and brown, wavy hair trimmed short. He dresses casually and expresses his opinions casually. Sherri is also a psychologist, shorter than her husband, with dark red hair and huge, expressive eyes. Both are new to Christ, and both are seeking a deeper love and deeper motivation.

We meet at Cathy and Roger's house on a Thursday night. I have no idea what this is about.

✦ ✦ ✦

Harry, my friend at the Camel Club, once told me that *The Big Book* was a volume for elementary school kids but the Bible was a book for college students.

I believe that with all my soul.

The author of the book of Hebrews gives us our lecture for today. "Let us not give up meeting together, as some are in the habit of doing, but let us encourage one another."

I know, I know, this is quite the enlightening discovery. Friendships help. I've found the Holy Grail.

But true friendships, based not on self-fulfillment but on unconditional love, are what separates those who would allow us to go on killing ourselves rather than get involved and those who would intercede if the need arose. I believe God put these people in my life for a reason, and that reason is recovery.

I had read about half of the Bible before we had our first meeting; some of its concepts were difficult for me. I wanted experienced Bible cruisers to help me. I thought all of these people were. I felt humbled to be in their midst. I found out everyone was seeking the Lord as we were. And I was comforted by that.

Cathy, I later discovered, is head of worship at our church. Roger is lay leader. They are giving, wonderful people. They never looked down on me for what I had done in the past, as I thought any Christian who knew my secret would. I shared some of my past at the first meeting. I have no idea how a shy person who had always struggled with meeting people could have done that without the help of the Holy Spirit.

Perhaps because of that, we began an intimate relationship as a group at our first meeting. It would wane later, but not before we had done all the teaching we could do to that point.

We met weekly, taking turns finding scripture to be the subject of discussion. We then journaled, writing what we thought or felt about the scripture. We opened up to each other and to the Holy Spirit. With each week, we became closer. The hugs grew genuine and deep. I learned that you could trust others. I began to learn that you could open up without fear, that you could be honest, completely honest, deep-down and caringly honest without fear of reprisal or fear of what the others in the group thought about your idea or your feeling.

I learned that you could have friends who don't visit your house or play sports with you. You could have friends without popping a beer can or unscrewing the top to a whiskey bottle.

We had our differences. We still do. But what we have in common overshadows everything else. We believe. We're one in the body of Christ. That has helped us through departures, disease, and a quest to stoke the fire that had gone out of the faith.

From Cathy, who was diagnosed as having cancer in May but through faith and prayer proved to be without the dread disease late in the month, I learned about serving. She gives her time on a daily basis, joyfully. Though she has struggled with what turned out to be nerve damage in her head from a virus and is often dizzy and bedridden now, she continues to host our Bible studies. She is my best friend. And for the first time, I don't worry if I'm hers. I consider it a privilege just to know her, and I thank God for my meeting her. She is my recovery in many ways. I can only pray that God gives someone like her to everyone during the first year of recovery.

From Roger, I learned analytical skills. He studies the Bible, really studies it. He understands that true wisdom comes only from God and he displays both generosity and kindness even to strangers.

From Dorsey and Sherri, I learned to search. When they moved away it set me back for a while, but I finally decided they had served their purpose in my life and I let them go. I no longer analyze friendships. I revel in how much I love them, and though they have not called and may never again talk to me, I thank them for the time we had.

From Kalynn, I learned optimism in the face of trial. She was never, never down. She truly loved the Lord. After a while, I wanted to model myself after her.

It's important to find a group of friends, you can share your burden with. We can't be in this alone. We have God, but we have other needs that only humans can meet.

Ask, pray, request, persist. God will provide the nurturing, loving, encouraging support you must have. Jesus said he came to set brother against brother and mother against child, but he also brought a family of believers together.

What is the true love of a friend, the kind I still seek, the kind I still pray for and wait for as patiently as my alcoholic soul allows? Paul described it this way: "Love is patient, love is kind. It does not envy, it does not boast, it is not proud. It is not rude, it is not self-seeking, it is not easily angered, it keeps no record of wrongs. Love does not delight in evil but rejoices with the truth. It always protects, always trusts, always hopes, always perseveres. Love never fails."

Of this—unlike Thomas sitting there sipping wine and feeling so utterly despondent because of the loss of the greatest friend he could ever imagine happening, I have no doubt. Whether or not humanity itself fails me, I have a friend in Jesus.

What more could I want?

In the end, it's not what kind of friends you find, or even what kind of friends God puts into your life that is critical. The key is what kind of friend you are. If you're concerned about what they can give you at this point in the journey, you might be in trouble. It is so much more important to see what sort of friend you can be, with the Holy Spirit's help.

That simple test would have kept Thomas from having a nickname we all know well, wouldn't it?

CHAPTER 19

Guilty as Charged

But one thing I do: Forgetting what is behind and straining toward what is ahead, I press on toward the goal to win the prize for which God has called me heavenward in Jesus Christ.
—Philippians 3: 13-14

No matter where you are in your spiritual journey, no matter how many days, months, or years you've had sobriety or even Jesus in your life, you've either dealt with or are about to deal with guilt.

Let me tell you about mine, with the certain knowledge that this will help me more than it does you.

✦ ✦ ✦

It's 1983. Four days before Christmas. It's freezing in Reno, Nevada, but there has been no snow below the mountain level near Truckee, California, about forty miles up into the Sierras.

Jason has just turned four. He is small, but his imagination is big. His tastes run toward Jedi knights and silver and gold droids. He has flown out with Mama from Jackson to visit, for both his birthday and Christmas.

They are scheduled to leave on the 4:40 Delta flight through Dallas. We arrive at the airport in plenty of time. We have a sandwich at the terminal's grill, talk about the week he's been there, the time we went into the mountains, playing football in the backyard.

When they call for flight 241, Mama hugs me, tears forming in her eyes. Jason doesn't notice. I squat, pat his little head, grab him and pull him tightly toward my chest. I hug him with all my strength, hoping that it will last until summer when I will see him again. I've talked to him each weekend since I moved to Reno in April. I promise to remain on schedule. There will never be a weekend that we don't talk.

He's wearing a red shirt and black pants, carrying a parka. He walks down the aisle toward the airplane. He pauses at the gate, turns back toward me, smiles a gap-toothed grin and waves. I carry that wave with me into the terminal bar, choking back tears. I can't stand it. I can't.

Would someone please tell me what I did to deserve this? Would someone please tell me what I'm doing here? Would someone, somewhere give me back my boy?

I order a Bloody Mary, and gulp so deeply the cold of the ice hurts my teeth. I stare into the murky drink, regret and guilt filling me more quickly that the liquid ever could. I know that I will never forget that face, that moment; I will carry them with me forever.

✦ ✦ ✦

It's March 1981 and is the last weekend of my first marriage, for all intents and purposes.

We're having a party, setting up my wife's brother with a date. He has recently moved out of our apartment into his own, having stayed with us for three months.

We invite a friend from work and two young women from my wife's job. We're young, it's a Friday night. We are free, except for Jason, of course. Free to have fun. Free to drink.

And everyone is having drinks. I, of course, am having more than anyone else, but I'm under control. This is a period in which I drink a lot but can hold my liquor, as they say, or so I believe. I finish a fifth of Canadian Club and head merrily into the second bottle. There's plenty of laughter and small talk. My friend and I watch part of a basketball game in the Southeastern Conference tournament, Kentucky versus Ole Miss. This does not mean much to the three women nor to the brother-in-law, and they begin having a discussion about current events.

My friend and I pay little attention for much of the conversation. Then, at halftime, we try to join in. My brother-in-law is telling the young women that if anyone were to break into his house, he would feel he had the right to shoot them, even kill them.

I don't know why, but I find this whole line of talk funny and I laugh.

I don't believe in killing of any kind, really. I don't even like to fish or hunt (which was another point of contention with my father, who loved both).

We begin to talk, growing louder. I'm back in an argument with my father. My brother-in-law takes on the role of Daddy quite well. Eventually, he picks up his things and begins to storm out. My wife is mortified. I go after my brother-in-law, thinking to calm him, to get him back inside. As I grab his shoulder, he turns on me and threatens to kill me if I touch him again. Of course, he doesn't mean that. But I'm drunk. I have no rationality. I hear only "I'll kill you."

Next thing you know we're rolling around on the ground. He's bigger than I am and gets the early lead in the festivities, sitting on me and pounding my head. My wife streaks out of the apartment and yells at me to quit, which I find immensely funny, since I'm the one being beaten, as far as I can tell. I say something to the effect of "I'll be happy to."

The brother-in-law gets off me. But I'm drunk, and the blows have had little effect. I start again, completely crazed at this point. I scream terrible things at him. Words are my weapons. I question his ability to find work, to pay for a decent car. I use my position at the newspaper as a bludgeon.

I am all that is wrong with mankind, at its deepest and worst point.

I am out of control. Like the little girl in Stephen King's *Firestarter*, who would make fire start by thinking it, send it out in a wave and bring it back with a command from her mind, I let my anger and resentment of him in the moment completely wipe out all rationality.

The next day I am told to leave. Jason never lives with me again, only visits. I'm worse than Daddy ever was. At least he never left us.

✦ ✦ ✦

Looking back at my life, I regretted so much. For years I walked with guilt, talked with guilt, along the narrow way. I had thought I had to be perfect, because, when I was being raised, I had to be perfect to gain praise. And I felt I had to have praise.

When I was divorced, when I lost Jason, I crumbled. It's a real wonder that I survived. I had nothing to fall back on, in my narrow way of seeing it, except the drink.

It was the worst period of my life, without question. I pray there will never be anything comparable.

I drank each night. Once I drank so much that I awoke in the car, a glorious morning having dawned. I was outside my apartment with no idea where I had been or how I had gotten home.

I tried to explain everything to Jason, but it was difficult. I had to pick him up at a mall near where my ex-wife was staying with her brother. I couldn't even come into his apartment.

As the months after the breakup passed, leading into the divorce, I began to stabilize somewhat. But the divorce affected everything. Guilt caused me to make terrible decisions. I was so worried about my secret coming out that I agreed to everything any of the lawyers, hers or mine, asked.

Jason came over every other weekend. I knew so little about being a parent. I drank while he was there. I cried when he left. I believe I cried so much during this period that eventually the tears dried.

I had eight job offers from various newspapers across the country over the next year; I even spent three drunken months at *USA Today*. But until I accepted a position in Reno (mainly because Reno offered a month's bonus), I turned them all down because of Jason. I had left him, but I couldn't leave him.

So I moved to Reno. And hated almost every minute of it. Loneliness was my only friend during the time I was there. The thought of Jason ate at my insides.

I lasted only ten months there. Just two weeks after Jason returned home (and I hated thinking of it that way) for Christmas, I called the newspaper I had left and all but cried over the phone asking for a way to come back. I took a hundred-dollar-a-week cut in pay and left sports (the only thing I knew, really) for what turned out to be four years.

I came back humbled, all but out of the mainstream of the business, away from any future I thought I had.

But I could see Jason. Hold him. Throw a ball with him. I wasn't Daddy. I was better. I wasn't him. I wasn't going to be him. There had to be a way to make this all right. What did I do to put myself in this position? I'm not bad.

I'm not.

I'm.

✦ ✦ ✦

The Bible has a lot to say about guilt, both healthy and

unhealthy. And there is a difference. I couldn't see this for years, but I do now, praise God.

Consider David, the second king of Israel. I had several things in common with him: he had some successes over the years; he put a lot of faith in national contests; he had a bright child; and he sinned horribly. And, as I did, he nearly let guilt tear him apart.

"Blessed is he," David wrote, "whose transgressions are forgiven, whose sins are covered."

David had a woman problem, and it kept him from having the close relationship he had previously had with God. "Blessed is the man whose sin the Lord does not count against him." Well, sure. I'd like everyone—especially God—to forget that night in Reno I got so drunk that I walked nearly four hours before somehow finding myself at my apartment with my car still at the bar where I'd left it. "When I kept silent, my bones wasted away through all my groaning all day long. For day and night your hand was heavy upon me; my strength was sapped as in the heat of summer."

I knew David's feeling. My life was stopped, on hold, without hope. And hope is what keeps us going, keeps us sane.

David, unlike me, knew what to do about it. It took years, the love of a good woman, more children, Mickey Mantle and Garth Brooks, the lack of a base hit and AA to do for me what David did essentially by himself.

"Then I acknowledged my sin to you and did not cover up my iniquity. I said, 'I will confess my transgressions to the Lord'—and you forgave the guilt of my sin."

Forgave the guilt of his sin. Not just the sin, but the guilt of his sin.

Took it away. Washed it clean.

And this before Jesus. Before the Son of God came and took upon his broad back every sin of every person ever born, bore it without shame, without guilt, on a cross that was built for both humiliation and death.

Forgiveness, loss of guilt. All offered free of charge. I had to do nothing whatsoever except accept the gift.

And it took years, years, for me to even attempt to do so.

✦ ✦ ✦

My friend Cathy once asked me if I minded her telling someone about what had happened to me. She had kept my strictest confidence, she said. I surprised her with my answer. I have no shame in what I am. I have no guilt or shame left about what I did. I gave those to Christ. He bears up under them quite well. I didn't.

I can't change a single thing about what happened, what I did, so I don't concern myself with those events. That is not heartless, though it might sound that way to someone who doesn't understand.

I don't regret a single thing that I did, either. I accept each and every thing as God-driven. If I hadn't been divorced, I wouldn't have met, fallen deeply in love with and married Mary. I wouldn't have Shanna or Carrie, wouldn't have become sports editor of the largest paper in my home state, wouldn't have then been offered a job in New Orleans that has a health plan that pays for substance abuse treatment, wouldn't have gotten treatment which led me to AA which led me to God which led me to salvation.

I do wish Jason and I had been together all these lost years, but maybe he was saved something he didn't need. I do wish he were with me now that I have some inkling about how life is to be lived. I do wish we knew each other better.

But if you accept everything that Jesus offers, including his loving hand to lead the way, you accept that all the decisions are ultimately his. In exchange, the guilt can be someone else's.

I don't need a bit of it any more.

✦ ✦ ✦

Jason has had some emotional problems over the years. He's gifted, talented in ways I've only hoped to be. He was sixteen before we discussed the divorce much. He told me for the first time that had he thought that perhaps I left them because I didn't like him.

I told him he could not have been more wrong.

When in the early spring my ex-wife called with the news that Jason was having real problems in school and at home with his stepfather (they had had a screaming match and had thrown a couple of blows), I attacked the problem in the way I was being taught.

I asked the Bible group to pray for him. I talked to my sponsor about Jason, who told me, "You sure do like to claim credit for everything, don't you?" I asked him what he meant. He said, "You can't take credit for every problem he has. Sometimes, in spite of your best efforts, teenagers are teenagers. Whatever is troubling him might have absolutely nothing to do with you. Quit beating yourself up. Just love him. Just help him in the best way you can. Pray for strength for him, your wife, your ex-wife, her husband, and especially for Jason."

I did.

And I sent him money for a train trip down.

I picked him up at the station. He's big, like his maternal grandfather, tall (six feet one) and broad, like the man he knew as Papaw. He has curly hair he has always kept cut short, though he plays in a rock band. He's a talented artist, writer and musician. My ex-wife did the absolute best she could with him, I believe, and I thank God for it.

I drove him to one of the canals around here, parked the car on the side of the road, and walked with him to the edge. The weather was warm, not hot, and the canal across from us was the deep green of spring.

We watched the canal flow gently, carrying broken limbs and a few bits of debris down the way. We were silent for a while. I waited for him to speak. This was his chance.

But you can't make someone talk. I tried to bring him out. I no longer needed alcohol to look inside myself, to speak from the heart.

I took the opportunity to explain as well as God would allow me what Christ had done for me. I told him that I wasn't sure his mother and I would have made it even if I hadn't been drinking. I said that I was 95 percent certain that if I hadn't been drinking so much in the first place we wouldn't ever have married. Don't misunderstand, I told him; I wasn't knocking her in any way. It was just that I didn't believe we were ever supposed to be married. But I was so lonely, as the friends I had grown up with were getting married, I was so into whiskey already, and I was so impatient to get on with life that I went into marriage recklessly. I had no background for marriage, no maturity, no level of patience. I was my father's son with all that that meant. I thought it was a woman's job to pick up around the apartment after her man. I thought decent table conversation included shouts when inevitable disagreements occurred. I thought it was a man's prerogative to have a few after-dinner drinks. If you couldn't win an argument, you could pound away on a wall, or maybe even threaten a slap or two. I thought I had run away from my father, and instead I turned into him. It takes more love than a person should have to give to put up with such. My first wife did it for four and a half years. My second wife, I told him, the right person, sent by God, to help me.

I told him he'd had nothing to do with what had happened. It wasn't all my fault, truthfully, but I accepted responsibility for everything wrong I did. I told him I'd been forgiven. I didn't worry about it any longer, and he didn't have to either.

I explained, carefully, slowly as that water drifted by us, as clouds floated so amazingly through the blue sky above us, how salvation works, how life in Christ isn't what he might imagine. If he was troubled, he could go to a psychiatrist, he could take medicine for it; I wasn't restricting him from that. But I told him that an author I trust, Max Lucado, wrote that if Jesus is one of your options, he is no option at all. He won't be taken half-heartedly, I told Jason.

We talked for about an hour, picked ourselves up, dusted off the grass and dirt from our pants and went home.

And I mean that in every sense of the word.

✦ ✦ ✦

Jason wrote the following letter to me. I offer it to every father with a problem of any kind with his child. It's never too late.

    Dear Dad:
    I'm writing you . . . inspired by your overcoming of alcohol. It felt so good to hear about it. It was something that your mind and body—self-consciousness and family did not need. Alcohol definitely did not get you Mary, me, Shanna, and Carrie. God, or maybe fate, gave you that. It seems as if you are becoming a new man and that fills me with so much warmth, that I feel renewed in my own life . . . .
    You've become the subject in one of Lazy Monday's (his band) new songs, "Dad Is Great." It's funk, almost disco, we kinda ripped off the name and beat from Bill Cosby—but oh well. He'll get over it. But alcohol has caused a lot of strife and misery in me. I've tried it once or twice and the only time I liked it was when it was a punch that was spiked and it was actually the punch I liked. So, I don't think I'll drink when I get older because (his stepfather) has given me a perfect example of what it'll do. Sure, maybe a beer or two at a party every once in a while, maybe those exceptions. But I doubt I will ever do it. I just don't want to bring myself down anymore. I want to lift myself above all the crap in the world. All the anger, loneliness, depression, regret,

emptiness, hate , crime, fear, everything that has held me down in my life. I want to get rid of it.

Dad, I want to be pure and free and so full of love that keeping a smile off of my face would be impossible. I also want to become close to you . . . know you inside, out . . . because I feel I barely know you . . . I want you to open up, let me in . . . give me half your heart. I'll give half mine, let you in . . . I need you to be my best friend right now . . . and as for me, never living with you again . . . don't count that out. I've still got college to go and I'm still not decided on which one to go to . . .

KEEP FIGHTING THE POISONOUS DRINK

I have faith in you and God to help you

JASON

You have no time for unhealthy guilt if you are spending your time praising God.

CHAPTER 20

Journal 9
March 1-April 10

Day 215, March 1
Sometimes I have bad days—or days when I feel bad inside because I can't relax. I can't quit moving, reading, doing, though I know that I can't save myself. I don't feel I'm doing enough. Enough what? I don't have a clue. I can't be good enough to please God. But I keep trying even though I'm not sure I should even be trying. Confusing? Well, now that you mention it.

Day 216, March 2
Dorsey and Sherri are looking at moving away. That would be a loss to the church. It would be a greater loss to me.

Day 224, March 10
Mississippi State wins the SEC basketball tournament. Miracles do happen.

Day 225, March 11
I'm tired physically, but my routines remain the same, which I believe is important. I begin each morning with prayer, reading, and journaling and complete each evening with the same, looking back at what I did right and wrong and asking God for

strength and courage to correct those faults. I ask for forgiveness and try again. It's quite a release to understand that I can never really succeed at this, but by grace I am deemed perfect by God. It erases all guilt and all worry when I let it work in me. When I get in the way, uh oh. The old way of living resurfaces. Human, huh?

Day 226, March 12

I've been asked to teach a class on the book of Acts. I've read it three times and have read a couple of studies of the book, so I guess I'm somewhat qualified. But I've never taught anything in my life, unless you count softball (as a coach). This should be interesting.

Day 228, March 14

Bible study:
The other day, Sunday, after Mississippi State beat Kentucky to win the SEC title, I was bouncing off the wall. My boss said something in the office to me that startled me at first. He said it was good to see me excited about something again. I thought about that statement for days until today. I told him it was quite a compliment. He didn't understand, as you probably don't now. Let me explain: I've never had much emotional balance. Little things would depress me. I could get motivated and turn impossible tasks at work into done deeds through sheer human drive. But the next day, the next week, as sure as day follows night, the bottom would fall out. But since I've re-asked Christ into my life, those hills and valleys have all but disappeared. Oh, there's the occasional one. But even those go away as I remember to let God deal with the problem. I know how to be abased, and I'm learning how to love as God's grace and my faith and understanding of that grace grows.

Sherri and Dorsey's leaving could be a real setback for me. I've really counted on this group as my anchor. And to quote Dorsey, the dynamics of the group has changed with their leaving. Sure, it's selfish, and I'll ask for forgiveness for the feeling, but I needed them a lot more than they needed me. And I'm scared. Scared about the future of the group and scared about my future. I counted on them. My hope—my true hope—is that God has done this for a reason. And I accept what I cannot change. I've learned this the hard way. But this is hard. I'm not very balanced at the moment, though for the good of the group I know "we can do all things through Christ who strengthens me." Although right now I feel like the man who said, "I believe. Lord, help me with my unbelief."

Day 229, March 15
Sherri is gone. One less friend. It's a loss. That's all I can say, really.

Day 231, March 17
Day follows night. Time passes. I feel better. Sherri is still gone, but she sure helped me when she was here. I hope I helped her. I should know that it ain't love unless you give it away.

Day 232, March 18
"Finding God in this life does not mean building a house in a land of no storms; rather, it means building a house that no storm can destroy."
—Finding God, Larry Crabb

Day 236, March 22
One thing I've noticed changing is my all-consuming need to be doing something. I still am getting a lot done, but I have more moments of quiet. And I like it. I need to continue to watch spending so much time in the bedroom away from the family. That was a habit that had been broken that I don't need to get back into, even if it's reading the Bible.

Day 238, March 24

I admit it. I'm tired. No doubt. Eight straight days of work does it to you.

But "let us not grow weary while doing good, for in due season we shall reap if we do not lose heart." (Galatians 6:9)

Day 240, March 26

I must tell my boss to watch his negativity. It affects not only him but me and the rest of the department. He's so talented that it sometimes is hard for him to relate to the rest of us, to understand why we can't do what he dreams of. It's a simple procedure, really. Think negative thoughts all the time—deserved or warranted or not—and you'll feel bad. Trust in the Lord that His plans are good for you, that there is a reason and He is in control, and be positive. What do you receive? Peace. From that peace, sometimes you get joy by the handfuls. I happen to think it's a pretty good bargain.

Day 244, March 30

A plan for perseverance:

1) Decide what you're committed to; 2) outline your goals; 3) plan out the steps you will need to take to reach your goals; 4) accomplish one step and then reward yourself; 5) recognize what part is in your hands and what is in God's; 6) expect God to inspire you with ideas; 7) evaluate, refine, try again; 8) refuse to give up except in the face of truth and honor or good sense. (*You Can*, Dr. Frank Minirith)

Calvin Coolidge said that nothing in the world can take the place of persistence. "Talent will not; nothing is more common than unsuccessful men with talent. Genius will not; unrewarded genius is almost a proverb. Education will not; the world is full of educated derelicts. Persistence and determination alone are omnipotent."

I would add a sovereign God who grants us persistence as a fruit of the Spirit.

Day 245, March 31
Mississippi State played poorly and lost in the Final Four. But, after some initial distress (it's the first thing a team of mine has lost since I sobered up; I kind of thought this meant I would win everything from now on), I was okay. It's better to take your best shot and fail than not take a shot.

Day 246, April 1
"Perhaps the greatest discovery of this century is that if you can change your attitude, you can change your life." (*Joshua*, Joseph F. Girzone)

Day 247, April 2
I sometimes wonder about why I was healed of the compulsion to drink, and I hear so many talk about needing a meeting. Lee, a good person with a law degree, a seemingly gentle man with great spirituality and meekness, goes to meetings almost every day, goes to two different step studies, etc. I believe my method—study and prayer, not to be grandiose to my fellows but to keep the Word of God always in my view—works for me. I question some of the methods of the twelve steps. In order to be more inclusive, the steps compromise who God is. That's a problem, a major problem for me. But as I've read recently, religion isn't about laws or commandments or steps, it's about people and spirit and heart. It isn't legalism, it's faith in God to remove those defects that have placed me in this position, even to have faith and gratitude for the lesson learned because of it. I'm learning discipline merely through my daily use of this notebook.

Day 248, April 3
Jesus' last week was full of courage. Do I have that courage without God's help? Doubtful at best. I wonder if I have that courage even with God's help.

Day 252, April 7 (Easter)
I'm tired. Saturday night was a wash. I did nothing. I felt bad. I don't feel like I should. The emotion for my Lord isn't here. Why? I have no idea.

Day 254, April 9
I have this urge to be anywhere but at work. I need motivation I can't find for the work.

Day 255, April 10
First softball tryouts today. I'm the head coach this year. It scares me to think that this is part of my old self. I hope nothing else returns of my old self.

Jason is not doing well. Suzie called and basically said he is one troubled youth. She suspects he's taken medicine that wasn't prescribed for him. He's cursed at her in a fit of anger, he's not sleeping at night, he's flunking, he's unhappy. My God. He needs help I am not fit to give. But my prayers will be very much for him tonight.

What do we do if Jason has a drug problem or something? Where do we go for help?

Can you believe I just wrote that? What has this whole journey been about? I believe I have a bit of expertise in this field. I'm such an idiot.

Panic does this to me, I guess.

I love him so much.

CHAPTER 21

Diamonds Are A Girl's Best Friend

Set your minds on things above, not on earthly things. For you died and your life is now hidden with Christ in God.
—Colossians 3:3

It's 7:13 p.m., Tuesday, a June evening in 1995.

My softball team, the team I coach, is playing in the Jefferson Parish West Bank tournament. We've already won two games in the tournament and lost one. One more loss and we're done with our season.

It's the sixth and final inning. We lead 7-5. We're pitching a thirteen-year-old girl. The league is for thirteen-to fifteen-year-olds. We've had to pitch thirteen-year-olds all season. This particular girl is going to be very good one day. She has struggled all season, however. Until tonight. This night she's pitching well. She's throwing strikes. But she's tiring.

We have only nine players, because we've lost four players to season-ending injuries. That is an unbelievable amount. But the loss of the players has brought us closer together, maybe even caused us to be better than we actually are, somehow.

Three outs and we will have beaten a team that defeated us twice when we had all our players.

We walk the first batter of the inning, bringing the tying run to the plate with nobody out. The next hitter slashes a sinking line drive toward shortstop. Shanna is playing there for the first time this season, because the girl pitching is normally our shortstop. Shanna makes the catch at her shoe tops, pivots quickly, and throws to second base to complete the double play. We're an out from at least fourth place in a ten-team league tournament. We'd finished seventh in the regular season with a nearly full complement of players.

We walk a batter. Then Shanna makes an error. They hit a ball to third base that our third baseman fields. I'm thinking about who to pitch the next night. But somehow the runner from second and the third baseman arrive at third base at the same moment, and our fielder drops the ball. Bases loaded.

No problem. Just need an out.

We walk in a run.

No problem. Just need an out.

We make another error on a ball that should have been caught. They tie the game.

I have done all I can with our little pitcher. I feel she's done. I take her out, bringing in a girl who doesn't throw hard but normally is pretty near the plate.

She walks in the go-ahead run.

We get an out, but the score is 8-7.

We bat in the bottom of the inning. We strike out. We strike out. Two outs and Melanie is at the plate, our catcher, our hottest hitter. Shanna will follow. Shanna is as cold as a jealous woman's stare. She has one hit in four games at the tournament. I've moved her from her normal third in the lineup to fifth. Usually I would be praying for Melanie to get on so Shanna could follow with the inevitable tying hit.

Tonight, in the third-base coach's box, I'm praying for Melanie to hit a home run. Shanna's stride is off. She's been taking a huge step with her front foot, which causes her to lose her balance when she swings. We've told her, but it hasn't helped. Sometimes these things just take time.

Melanie slams one to right-center. The ball slides between two outfielders, bouncing low off the chain-link fence that surrounds the field. She rounds first and chugs toward second. I'm throwing my hands in the air as she rounds second. She is in secure scoring position at second with two out. Of this, I am sure.

She rounds second, her stocky legs churning (she has a catcher's speed). She's coming toward me. I see the ball relayed to their shortstop. She has no chance whatsoever of getting to third before the ball arrives. I can only hope for a bad relay.

The ball zips past Melanie's blonde head into the third baseman's glove. The girl applies the tag to the sliding Melanie, ending the inning, the game, and our season.

Shanna is left standing in the on-deck circle. Part of me is hurt. Part of me is happy it wasn't Shanna who failed.

I walk into the dugout, in a daze. I'm not sure I know why Melanie didn't stop at second. A father, the father of the pitcher I've taken out of the game, comes up to the fence of the dugout. He screams at me. I ask, "What did I do?" I really have no idea what I have done to deserve this. "Nothing," he says. "That's the problem. You did nothing. All season. You were just a body."

We pick up our equipment and clear out, leaving behind the last season I would coach Shanna. I walk over to a big oak tree near the entrance to the complex, where the team is waiting. I tell them how proud of them I am, how much each of them has meant to me, how what we did with nine players, five of whom were thirteen, was really something. My voice is quiet, soft, hurting.

I thought— well, I don't know what I thought. But I'm pretty sure I never imagined that I would make people angry if I coached the way coaching should be done. That had been my intent, my purpose in coaching the teenagers one more time. Was it worth it? I wondered even as I hugged and received hugs from the players.

No. It wasn't. But, God willing, I'll do it again for Carrie next summer.

✦ ✦ ✦

Sometime during your recovery, you're going to come face to face with something from your past, from your old way of being.

With me, it was softball and maybe barbecues. With you it might be a bar, a group of friends, a certain time of the day, a holiday.

Anything that tempts you to try to live the way you did before is dangerous. It takes prayer and effort on your part to get past these times.

When softball season came, I was worried about what the effect might be on my sobriety. It seems strange now to discuss that notion. But it was a real terror, despite all I had learned and all that God had done for me.

Softball, baseball really, was a way of life for me and my family, as much as something like playing the horses or working for the church. I learned to read by studying box scores in the local newspaper when I was five. I played from the time I was eight until I was thirty-five and my eyesight was poor enough to necessitate wearing glasses. I sweated so much that I couldn't play with my glasses on and I couldn't see without them. I retired to coach Shanna at that point.

She was eight. I have coached her, either as an assistant or as a head coach, each year since.

Sometimes I felt that was the only way we really communicated. But we did communicate about softball. She knows every rule, every strategy any boy could possibly know about the game. We've sat in front of Braves games talking strategy a number of nights.

She learned the rules: A player is always on time, never misses practices, plays hurt, admits mistakes by saying "my fault," then forgets the error. A player is always a team player. The team is the most important thing there is. Nothing fragments the team.

All this she was taught.

And as my spiritual journey continued through the year, I questioned every bit of it. I was coaching a youth team. This only became apparent to me when I sobered up. Before, it was about my knowledge of the game, my ability to coach, to organize. It was about me.

I gave serious thought to the question of whether I should coach again.

I decided that I would coach, but I would do it the right way. Winning would come as a result of good, fun practice. I wouldn't care about the wins and losses, but only the improvement of the players. I wouldn't yell at any player, ever, no matter what the problem was. Teaching would be the most important job I would have. If they knew the game, truly knew the game when the season was over, then I would have done a good job.

All this I pondered before the season began.

The only problem was that no one else—not the team, not my assistants, especially not the parents—thought about it in the same way I did.

The softball season was merely symbolic for any number of situations a person might face. It's a kid's game, but it's a segment of life that must be faced. Life must be handled on life's terms. And I had to cope with it, or drink again. It was that serious.

✦ ✦ ✦

We finished two games below .500, my first losing season as a coach. But the adversity we faced was well above 500 percent. And we learned so much together.

We faced problems together. One player, Heather, had much the same background I did. Her father and mother were divorced, and both had drinking problems. I remember one time talking with her about God. She'd gone to a spiritual retreat and missed the pre-season tournament. After her return, she had a problem at one of the games with her father, who usually came there with a large beer stashed in his pocket. She was down, bitter about her father watching most of her brother's game but not being at hers. I asked her if she felt she had learned much at the spiritual retreat, or had she gone there to play? She said she had learned. I told her not to forget whatever lesson she had absorbed there. "God doesn't stop helping you just because you left the spiritual retreat," I told her. She smiled, and went back to the game. I felt so sad for her, and was even more grateful for what God had done for our family.

We faced bad games together. We seemed to come ready to play only every other game. I don't know why.

We went through the good times together, screaming after an amazing ten-run final at-bat to beat one team.

We grew together as coaches. We had one older assistant whose way of coaching was to bellow at the players. The players took umbrage at this and talked about him behind his back. But at the next-to-last game of the season, it was he who bought birthday cakes for the five girls who'd had birthdays during the season.

We faced adversity together. We had three ankle turns, one accident off the softball field in which one of the girls put her arm through a glass door, and a broken thumb.

Through it all we competed, grew, played better, played worse.

We played, to coin a baseball term, by the book. By God's book. As usual, it came down to one final game, one final night. One final extension of ourselves as individual players and as a team.

✦ ✦ ✦

In a perfect world, the game would be the thing. There

would be no parents using coaches as babysitters; there would be no sad kids. Everyone would move all over the field, learning each position. There would be no haves and have-nots. There would be no concern about the final score, only about how the kids were learning, how they were progressing, how close they were getting to the best they could be.

In the world that God did not create, there are parents who come only to the games, scream at coaches who are doing what they feel is necessary for the children, and offer no help. There is a win-at-all-cost attitude, no matter what harm is done.

For example, one time a coach came up to protest the game, potentially causing us to forfeit, because we weren't wearing chin straps on our helmets. Granted, we should have been. It was a rule I should have known about. But to cause a group of kids to lose a game because of that? The coach would have to tell his team that even though they didn't play well, they won, not because of anything they did, but because they had an observant coach.

I'm not saying winning or losing isn't important. As long as they keep score, it will have some importance. But it isn't the greatest thing; the game is.

And learning to be your best. Learning to focus, to carry yourself as a winner. Learning to be the best God would have you be.

According to the best definition of sin I read during that year, it is anything that keeps us from being what God wants us to be, and that's the best we can be. God's plan might be for us to be mediocre, average. We must be content with that plan if doing His will is an important in our lives as it should be, must be, if we're to be full of His peace.

✦ ✦ ✦

Before the last game we played, I walked around the outfield fence, looking in at my team warming up. I thought only of the good parts of the season, not the injuries, the hurt feelings. I thought of all of Shanna's seasons, and I smiled. It is never easy, raising children, at any stage of their lives. But it is worth the effort. Sometimes you can help them. Sometimes you can't.

But I guarantee that the closer you are to your children, which you absolutely can't be if you're drunk, the better your life will be. That's what this spiritual journey is all about. I wanted to be a better person. I wanted to find happiness. And once I found it, I wanted to give it away.

CHAPTER 22

Journal 10
April 11-29

Day 256, April 11

I must get back on track. I didn't sleep much worrying about Jason. But it's good that Suzie and I are talking. Perhaps that is the benefit of Jason's problems.

Day 257, April 12

We talked to Dorsey about Jason, and he suggested asking about the medicine he was taking. Not sleeping, Dorsey said, is a sign of depression. Erratic behavior is a possible sign of drug use. Taking medicine is a sign of a problem, if he did this. "The kid obviously has a story to tell," Dorsey said. "And if the story isn't being told to whomever he's seeing, he needs to see someone else. He might be helped by a change in environment because of the unique circumstances of the opportunity of two households. Finally, you need to be really careful about the signs of depression, because teenage suicide is so prevalent. It's a difficult time as a rule, and if he's deeply troubled by a relationship or environment, you must be very careful. Support his independence without giving him too much liberty. Working during the school week might be too much for him."

Day 258, April 13
We made final cuts for my softball team. It didn't go well, because we cut a player who was talented but who we thought might be more trouble than we needed as coaches. Three girls called, wanting desperately to be on the team. I hated telling them they simply weren't quite as good as the players who made the team. I'm not sure I ever want to do anything like that again.

Day 259, April 14
Mary talked to Jason today after his concert, and he seemed happy. Thank God.

Day 260, April 15
"The Lord said: 'Surely I will deliver you for a good purpose; surely I will make your enemies plead with you in times of disaster and times of distress.'" (Jeremiah 15:11)

Day 261, April 16
Practice makes imperfect, at least the softball team must think so.

Day 262, April 17
Practice tonight was rained out, sort of. We talked. Just talked. The thirteen-to-fifteen year-old team is difficult sometimes. Quite frankly, I'm not having that much fun. We have one girl who is up one night, down the other. I'm concerned about her mood swings. I don't know how long this can go on. Is it worth it trying to keep her happy? I don't know. I suspect it is if I'm going to coach this team, teach this team in the principles I want them to learn. It's just a game, and this young woman has many bigger problems than playing softball.

Day 264, April 19
We talked tonight during practice about thinking about success. If you think you're going to fail, you're going to. If you can

visualize success, you can make it happen. I had an opportunity to witness about where strength comes from and I failed to speak up.

Day 266, April 21
"John teaches us that the strongest relationship with Christ may not necessarily be a complicated one. He teaches us that the greatest webs of loyalty are spun, not with airtight theologies or foolproof philosophies, but with friendships, stubborn, selfless joyful friendships." (*No Wonder They Call Him the Savior*, Max Lucado)

Day 268, April 23
To Dorsey: From the time I was eight years old, I knew exactly what I wanted to be. I wanted to be great. It didn't really matter at what. I wanted to be great. To be remembered. I read autobiographies so I could find out what they would ask me. Thirty-three years later I finally decided the biographies on the Arts and Entertainment channel probably hadn't lost my phone number. They weren't going to call. But my opinion of what "great" means has changed. I now feel, because of the Spirit living in me, that all we can truly hope for is to affect someone else. Someone's life, someone's heart. God willing, someone's soul. It's the goal. The pot of gold at the end of Noah's rainbow. It's the best. Dorsey, you will be remembered, of that I am certain. Because you chose to openly, honestly say what you felt in all matters. What the Holy Spirit led you to say. You chose to love, rather than be loved. But in that choosing, we were moved to love our brother and remember. That alone makes me feel great.
God bless you and keep you, Dorsey.

Day 269, April 24
I need to take softball less seriously. I coach and teach to the best of my knowledge and ability and the girls have it from there. Ultimately, how do I make it fun but challenging?

Day 271, April 26
Can you be successful in sports if you truly don't care about the outcome of the game but instead care about the performance itself? Beats me.

Day 272, April 27
What is worry? Anything that drains your tank of joy. Something you can't change. What do I have to worry about? We've had more tension in this house this week. Why? Little things that pull us out of the peace God intends for us to have. Remember balance. Strive for the middle ground and love the girls. That is enough.

Day 273, April 28
How great is God? We're allowed to call on Him in our homes, our cars, our bathrooms if the need to talk arises. And the inner glow that comes from my daily, hour-to-hour worship I hope, trust and pray shows what is written on my heart. If we accept the positive, spontaneous thoughts and feelings that occur and see that they stem from God, we will receive the guidance we need. All we need to do is listen, receive and act without fear. And make darn sure we aren't drunk, or we can't listen at all.

Day 274, April 29
Nine months ago, I drank a bottle of rum, and, God willing, it was my last drink. Through up times and down times, I've not drunk. The up times actually affect me more than the down. It's hard sometimes to enjoy a nice warm afternoon and know I can't have a cold beer. Other times it grieves me that I'm different. Being good sometimes just builds up like pressure. Weird, but true. I want people to depend on me, to be able to depend on me, to think I'm good, heck, I'm great. Then I always let them down. Before, my identity was tied to my job. Now, it's tied to my recovery, my weight loss, my religion. Am I doing all of this for praise? Why can't I love for love's sake? Why can't I just live?

CHAPTER 23

Journal 11
April 30-August 29

Day 276, April 30

I felt terrible today. I don't like the plan my boss has with me working 1-8:30 p.m. I felt like I'd failed, and I was questioning everything—my faith, my sobriety, everything.

But something clicked at practice. I felt better—still do. Who knows what any of this means? My boss said I wasn't the same person that I used to be—and he's right. I've thrown myself into everything—and accomplished nothing. But all is not lost. That's what faith is. Through the tough times—and they've been tough for over a week—understanding that they'll pass, understanding that even when I feel like giving up, everything, as long as I call for help, I'll receive.

Day 278, May 2
When God decides I'm ready to be anything, I'll be told.

Day 280, May 4
My first wife says what I'm doing may be affecting her husband. Oh, but that it would. If my quitting drinking, finding God would allow him to, that would be wonderful.

Day 285, May 9

We exist on fast food, both spiritual and physical, never taking enough time to slow and absorb. Mary and I rush to games, practices, Bible studies, AA meetings, work, home for homework, a quick bite, a quick prayer tossed out at the end of a quick day—and the Master of our lives, knower of all things, tells us to slow, take a sweet Holy breath and talk to our Father, alone, on your knees if it suits us. Feel the love, the quiet, absorb it, roll around in it like spring flowers. Take the stress and the hectic life, the head aches, the allergies and dump them on Him. Be free to smile, to love. Claim your freedom in Christ alone in solitude and ask for the peace of God that surpasses all understanding. If we reach a point where we just can't find a moment of respite from practice schedules, game lineups, church committee meetings, work budgets, AA chairmanships or the next quick lunch, remember that we serve a God of power, as well as love. And he will both reward our efforts to serve and give us strength to complete the commitment.

Day 287, May 11

We consciously slowed down tonight. We went to a movie, ate a steak, concentrated on being at peace. It comes hard to us. But we felt good.

Day 288, May 12

I've got to look at the positives. How?
1) greater prayer;
2) don't listen to those around me when they are negative;
3) concentrate on the positives in my life;
4) study His word more deeply.

Day 289, May 13

Not only should a coach and a father adjust to each individual player, each child, being honest with them, getting the most they have but adapting to their individual personalities, but he must adapt to the personality of the team. I'm finding the difficulty lies in MY desire to win, which may not be quite the same as the team's. My job is to motivate, as well as teach. And it is difficult, or has been so far, to fully reach them. They don't listen most of the time. But I can see little progress, little moments, bits and pieces. Can we make enough progress in the time we have? That's God's challenge for us.

"Fix these words of mine in your hearts and minds; tie them as symbols on your hands and bind them on your foreheads. Teach them to your children, talking about them when you sit at home and when you walk along the road; when you lie down and when you get up." (Deutcronomy 11: 18-19)

Day 294, May 18

Cathy has been diagnosed as potentially cancerous again.

Jason is still searching—still not getting home when he's supposed to.

Kalynn can't pull the trigger on a job.

Life is life, some hard, some understood, some not. Criminals, scum on street corners selling kids guns and drugs, not caring whose lives are taken. And Cathy might have cancer. Her daughter might have a tumor.

And life goes on.

Understanding why I've been saved from the clutches of alcoholism and Cathy would get cancer is too difficult to imagine.

But God's will be done.

It's what I cling to in the darkest night.

Day 298, May 22

Cathy doesn't have cancer. They ran tests designed to see how bad the cancer was. They were sure, absolutely stone-cold sure. But they neglected to take into account the sincere prayers of the believers.

Day 299, May 23

This is a process. My problem lies in wanting the process of becoming to be at my speed, my pace, in my time. I don't like the message found in Ephesians 6 for two reasons. I'm not sure I can do it. I'm not sure if there is any of this I can do. I am simply trusting as much of my total being as I can at a particular moment to God, and then I'm doing the reading of His word.

There are moments when I read a passage of scripture and I know I have it—whatever IT is, peace, sometimes joy, understanding, a sense that my life has purpose and meaning—and conversely there are times when that shield is battered by my lack of strength or Satan or a world that kills babies and endorses same-sex marriages or a world where my friends go through pain and a world where a 19-year-old UNO pitcher is killed in a car wreck and well, by the mystery of it all.

God's joy was what I sought when I began this journey, well, joy of some kind, not so and so's joy, nor Billy's joy, nor Mary's joy, nor even Kalynn's.

I find it. I really do, at times. And then, me being me, it slides away like a California home in the rainy season.

I believe God is the conductor and this world is His symphony. Sometimes however, my pride, ego and stupidity makes me want to grab the baton. Hey, let's do it my way, I shout into the unlistening winds. I never notice they're not listening.

Bible study is a moment to unclinch the teeth and loosen the jaw of life. I know again to be still and thank God without ceasing. The friends there are my salve to a self-inflicted wound. My wife, my friends and my Lord together in one room, thankful just to be breathing and worshiping.

I have so much to be grateful for again. If I can just, just slow down for a moment, be still and know He is GOD. All the doubts, discouragements and discourse will be washed away by His blood.

Unlike a newspaper, of this I can believe what I read.

Day 305, May 29
Ten months. I thank God for the time well spent.
Maturity: the ability and willingness to be led where you would rather not go.

Day 307, May 31
I see people like Kalynn and mother crying in their love for the Lord and I don't. I envy them so much. Why can't I feel? I try to show Christ my gratitude. I try to feel it like skin. But I fail.

Day 311, June 4
I can't take much like this:
My first wife called this morning. She said that Jason failed Algebra II. He must make up the work this summer.
One of the girls broke her thumb at last night's game.
Cathy and Roger called, and just writing this is about more than I can manage. Apparently Cathy has a diagnosis of cancer in the bones of her head. Just like that. She's potentially terminal. A month ago, she wasn't even sick.
What was all this journey for if this is the result?
All I have left is trust. I either trust in what I read in the Bible or I don't. And I'm trying hard to trust. It's easy to see: Either this is the answer or there are NO answers. Nothing in life makes sense or is usable. And I get drunk.
That's not what I either want or will allow, if God is with me.

Day 314, June 5
I think I feel worse than Cathy does. Says something about the selfishness still festering in me, doesn't it?
"I will lift up my eyes to the hills, from whence comes my help." (Psalms 12: 1)
When the darkness threatens to surround us, I believe some people, who have matured in Christ enough, have the ability to

thank God for the lesson to be learned. I'm so immature I just question, doubt and wonder. God grant me time, just time.

Day 314, June 7

My boss says I'm floating. I need to find my concentration, he said.

My best friend, my anchor point in Christ, my mentor is dying. My son is failing, and I don't know how much of that is my responsibility.

I'm not floating. I'm sinking.

Day 314, June 7

When do I sigh?

When Shanna talks on the phone and spends all her time in her room away from us. They tell me this is typical teenager-dom. I dislike it.

When Carries leaves a pack of cookies open in front of the TV, and Scrappy eats them.

When Cathy stares down her mortality and sees bleakness instead of joy, and I join her all too quickly instead of helping her.

When Mom sees 70 years of age as a barrier she'd rather not cross.

When Mary can't get rid of her allergies.

When kids across this city keep killing themselves instead of talking about the problem.

When I fall to temptation, although I understand as well as anyone where to go for help.

When things don't go the way I believe they should.

When I see lonely, desperate people worrying about their ordinary, unfulfilled lives and suddenly realize I'm one of THEM.

Day 315, June 8

Cathy called. My GOD, it's not cancer. It's not fatal. It's not. It's not. Praise God. Prayer again knocks the big C out of the park. I'm not on the roller coaster again, but I can see the monster in the foreground.

Day 232, June 16

It's Father's Day. I got a card, a beautiful Christ-themed baseball shirt. And the love of some beautiful kids. All my life I wanted a father to put my arms around, to tell me I did something good, to smile at my hits and comfort me on my misses.

To learn from, maybe to praise and watch a frown turn into a sparkling grin. I never had that, and it drove me to the edge of a canyon from which there would have been no return. But my mistake was trusting in my adopted parents and what I learned from my earthly father instead of my Father in heaven. I can't send a card today, but I send my love to Him who puts His arms around me when I'm down, corrects me when I'm wrong and smiles broadly those few times I'm right.

Happy Father's Day, Lord.

With love,

Billy or Peter or whoever I am.

Day 327, June 20

The apostle Paul spent the majority of his life with sincere, great focus on three things. God does what He does by grace; I am what I am by the grace of God; I let YOU be what YOU are by the grace of God.

Like a peanut butter sandwich is simple but as great an invention as man has made, so is the doctrine of grace.

Carrie asked to miss a softball game tomorrow night in order to go to the final day of vacation Bible school. I surprised myself and her by saying yes. Of course, I can't believe she asked.

When the Lord moves, you better be ready. Great things do happen.

Day 329, June 22

We live in an era where we're told to be like Mike. Where

winning is the only thing. Our movie heroes are Stallone, Willis. Who never lose the battle. Who never die. Where self-help books sell by the millions. Where people actually make livings giving speeches about motivation.

Jesus tells me that the truth will set me free. The truth is that For what the law was powerless to do . . . God did.

I accept that God has plans for me. I accept that God wants me to work toward being the absolute best I can be.

When will the difficulty of the spiritual journey be over? When I can accept that what God wants for me could be mediocrity, but being helpful to others. In other words, when can I accept that maybe God doesn't plan for me to be great? That I won't get that job I wanted, or my kids won't be the first women to play for the Braves, or we will never have that house in the country with the white-picket fence as the border of the property.

When I reach the stage that Paul did, imprisoned but content.

Then, only then, will peace completely surround me, envelope me like a mist.

Trust in God means believing that will come. And, unbelievably, I believe it will.

Day 331, June 24

I didn't go to AA tonight. I might not go again. Wrong or right, my faith is in Christ, not AA. I want to spend the time with my family and it's a growing family of Christ. If I return, it will be merely to help, to witness for Christ. I don't know where I'm headed, but this is the answer to many prayers about the subject, I believe. It might be dangerous, but I don't believe God will let me drink again. My sponsor once said that the primary purpose of AA, the only reason it exists, is the problem of alcohol. I believe that God is the reason I exist, and that the problem of alcohol was but his way of reminding me of that fact.

Jesus says he is the only way to the Father. You must go through him to reach the Father. So, since witnessing for Christ is not appreciated at AA, in order that the program remain inclusive (which I understand), I can't support it any longer. I have empathy for all alcoholics, suffering and dying slowly but surely, as I do for all Moslems, Jews and unbelievers everywhere. I have to go beyond sobriety, I must.

But Christ is my rock, upon which my life must be built.

So the journey heads in a slightly different direction. But moves all the more.

Day 342, July 5

Perhaps all of this journey was for just this purpose. I need all the patience, inherent love and wisdom to help solve the biggest problem we've had since I quit popping tops.

Shanna is on the all-star team, again. She is starting in left field. She, for six months, has been practicing for a dance that will celebrate her best friend's 15th birthday, a Spanish tradition I'm told.

Tonight Shanna brought to our attention that she is irreplaceable at that dance. I had told her months ago that she could go only if there was no conflict with softball. And I told her to tell her friend and her friend's mom this detail.

The dance, reception, whatever is scheduled, I'm now told, a week from tonight, the night of the district championship. Her friend's mom has been calling Shanna, putting extreme pressure on her. She can't do both. She's in a terrible fix, albeit of her own doing. And I probably made it worse by saying a lot of mess at her for the second straight night.

Mary broke down in tears.

Shanna, miss coldness, miss I'm in my room on the phone if you need me, cried on my shoulder for the first time since I've been sober.

I have done nothing, right or wrong, to help or hurt this situation. And I have no solutions. Nothing to offer. Sometimes we can just listen. Sometimes the problem is bigger than Daddy can be.

If Shanna felt she could talk to us more, about both good and bad, perhaps it wouldn't have reached this stage before we knew it was this big a problem.

Softball is important. It is. But it isn't worth this. Not the hurt that has gone into it, into our family this summer.

1) Mary getting mad at Carrie's coach and actually saying something to him about where Carrie was batting, which is against everything I always believed in;

2) Her coach, in response, moving Carrie in the lineup to ninth, past several younger girls with no idea about what game they were even playing, which led Carrie to sob on the bench during the first inning of a game, feeling more of a failure than any little person should ever be made to feel;

3) Me being screamed at for trying to do my best, but not enough to suit a particular father;

4) Carrie being passed over for all-stars in favor of an assistant coach's daughter who had one hit all season;

5) Shanna coming face-to-face with a slump for the first time, going 4-for-her-last-29 at bats, failing miserably in the post-season tournament;

6) Finally, Mary crying. That's too much. That's the end.

Why? For what? So I can relive my youth. This isn't 1968. That's over. It'll never be again. This isn't Meridian versus Northeast. That will never be again. Why can't they just have fun?

None of this has anything to do with the Lord. But it's my life. And that is the crux of the matter. When anything, softball or baseball or the Braves or smoking or whatever, becomes more important than the Lord, the wheels run off the vehicle and the journey slows to a crawl. Or if you let it, to a halt.

But I remember what I've been taught. I'll take this whole thing to God in prayer. And the answer will bring back the smiles for everyone. If they believed the way I do.

Day 346, July 9

What did I want out of life that made me begin the journey

that still has me hungry for righteousness? I wasn't filled. I didn't think I was a good example for my kids. I didn't love my wife as fully as I could or should. My health was questionable. I didn't feel I had ever given 100 percent to anything.

I remember nights of my youth, simple nights. Warm but pleasant summer nights. We'd sit out on the porch in old, faded aluminum chairs, with rust running up the sides. The sticky nights were cut by laughter and street lights at Aunt Juanita's. Sometime during the early evening, the fog machine, an old truck with two sprayers for mosquitoes on the back, would come bumping down rough, beat up 39th street, up from Highland Park and the little league fields. The kids would run behind the truck, screaming, acting like crazy people, waving our arms to stir the clouds of insecticide. Later, we'd slice fresh, ripened watermelon and spit the seeds anywhere we wanted. Often I'd sleep at my aunt's and drift off to a blast of air sucked in by her huge attic fan.

I wanted those days to return. Times when the weight of responsibility wasn't crushing me. Times when I knew the next morning, when I awoke, I wouldn't have times to be places, schedules to keep, meetings to attend. Times when the hardest decision of the day was whether Rickey was going to throw a curve or a fastball. Times when house payments and philosophical dilemmas weren't suffocating. Times when life wasn't a pressure cooker and I wasn't a green bean out of Mama's garden.

I longed for simplicity.

I longed for someone, somewhere, to take this burden away.

I discovered that Jesus would, but there is a little price that must be paid.

I had to grow up.

They told me in the beginning that alcoholics' maturity often freezes at the point they begin drinking. So, I'm really a teenager.

And now, in the first year of new growth, I've come face to face with a teenager's problems. Mine and Jason's and Shanna's. And the weight of the problems is bending my back so terribly,

I'd break if Jesus weren't with me to hold me and whisper so gently but so compellingly that I have help.

Shanna is much more mature than I am, it hurts and makes me proud at the same time.

She called her all-star coach and told him she'd be missing the game. She was responsible, she explained her decision and he accepted it.

I don't know if she's learned anything from me over the years, but I am learning from her.

Thanks God. I am blessed. I understand that blessings sometimes come in blonde packages.

Day 349, July 12

Bad day in Terrytown. Let me see if I understand all that has happened.

I awoke to find that Shanna's friend had called. Shanna didn't go to the dress rehearsal last night because her team was playing in the semifinals. There was never, to my understanding, a discussion about her missing two games. Her friend's mother has been calling telling Shanna first that she wasn't going to be able to be in the dance and reception because of this miss. Then after I made the mistake of calling her coach to tell him what I saw as good news, the mother called back many times to make sure Shanna was going to be at the dance.

We struggled with decisions all morning. What to do? What to do?

On the clock, I told Mary and Shanna that I was going into the bedroom and pray. As soon as I hit my knees, God spoke to me. I received an image of Shanna writing a note to her team, wishing them the best, hoping for a victory in tonight's finals that would send them to the state tournament again. Shanna accepted that decision, wrote a nice little note, called her coach back and explained everything, took the note over to one of her teammates' house.

I thought that was the finish.

Not in the Turner household.

At 6:05 p.m., five minutes after the scheduled game time, the same father who screamed at me at the season's end, called. He was on a cell phone and all I heard him ask was, was it true Shanna wasn't coming to the game? I answered yes, thought about going into how difficult this had been on all of us, and thought better of it. He said, harshly, "That's all I wanted to know." End of conversation.

Shanna went to the dance and reception. At least that's over.

Day 350, July 13

I received a call from the news copy desk when we got home from Bible study about 10:30 p.m. They had pictures from the championship game. They asked me if I knew who had won. I explained that any other time I would know, but not this night. I told them that maybe they could call the ballpark, and gave them the number, saying I didn't think there would be anyone there. But they told me they understood that the game had been delayed.

I thought nothing more of it, and went to bed, happy that this entire episode was past us, hoping Shanna's team had won so I could see her play some more.

The next morning, I opened the newspaper to find on the cover of the Metro section a cutline stating, "Players from the West Bank East and the West Bank West softball teams waited patiently as coaches and officials tried to decide whether the West Bank East team would have to FORFEIT the Dixie Belles championship tournament Friday because A PLAYER WAS MISSING."

Ughhhhhhhhhhhhhhhhhhhhhh!

The old self that was me regarded forfeits as the worst scourge of mankind. Losses I could almost stand. Forfeits, no way.

"Peace I leave with you. My peace I give to you." (John 14: 27)

Day 351, July 14

We sorted out all the details. An obscure rule about all

players on the team, if not injured, having to be at every game played in a tournament was the focus of the dispute. They finally played, and lost. Shanna lost, too. Because of the dishonesty she displayed at times during the affair, we took away her phone line, which was like taking away her breath.

Word around the ball parks is that I knew this was a rule and didn't care.

But if I've learned anything during this year it's that what people think of me is of little importance. Pleasing God is my mission, and I think he gave me greater patience than I could have hoped for in all of this.

Having said that, I can't tell you how great it is that softball is over.

Day 355, July 17

Bible study:

This life we lead is a series of knocks sometimes. I look at my wonderful wife and marvel at how I never, ever see her down or discouraged. I can't do that. I want to, need to, and am trying to let God work in me to reach that point. But to date, I can't. I don't accept that I will never learn to endure. I feel the shift, the slide toward endurance. His promises say I will. I want, hunger and thirst for the kind of righteousness that Paul had. But even after his conversion on the road to Damascus, he took three years of study and thought and prayer before he began his ministry with a trip to Jerusalem, after starts and missteps just days after the conversion.

It takes time. I realize and accept it.

Perhaps all I have right now is acceptance. That's okay. Never had it before.

But I hurt when nicked, still; I question. I wonder. I doubt. And, thank God, he picks me back up from the gutter of doubt and confusion I always fall into, and we continue, tiny step by tiny step, together.

Am I qualified to help others? I'm qualified to tell you stories of my sins, of my failures, of my excuses. And a little more each day of my acceptance of grace.

I now admit this really is a marathon. Or perhaps more important than admitting it is wanting it to be. I want a long life, if God wills it, to serve. I want to get out of myself and into the business of Christ. There are so many others out there that haven't heard, really heard, the Good News.

These daily mistakes of mine are just minute portions of the entire race. With God's sweet mercy, I'll have a great kick left at the end.

Or at least a heck of a party when the race is over and we go home.

If Jesus could endure the shame for all my many sins, the very least I can do is endure a few problems for his sake.

I'll try.

It is the best I have. But I believe God says it's enough.

Day 365, July 29

12:04 a.m.

A year. A whole year. I quit drinking for a year. And found Christ.

You know why it's so hard to find Christ, by the way? It's because he was never lost.

I was.

The fruits of the Spirit have begun to grow in me. Little blossoms are popping up all over. Mary is wonderful, a growing woman in Christ. Shanna and Carrie are happy, when fully separated from each other. (Again, they tell me this is normal.) Life is really great. I mean that. I've learned a bit about honesty, and I wouldn't lie about the greatness of God.

All because of Mickey Mantle, a few breaks and God's great loving grace.

It's been interesting, hard, easy, all those things. It's been the greatest year of my life. And God promises it will get better as Christ continues to remake me.

There's this thing about nicotine I need help with.

And the caffeine of Diet Cokes and coffee might be more than I need.

There are plenty of things left to do. Maybe break down my journal and see if there is a book there. Maybe I could help someone with what I've experienced.

Got to go.

There's a whole new year coming. I can't wait to see what Jesus has in store for me, Mary, the kids, and Mama. Oops, I'm patiently waiting to see.

Some things I might never learn, huh?

CHAPTER 24

Final Thoughts
(for now)

"Since we have these promises, dear friends, let us purify ourselves from everything that contaminates body and spirit."

—2 Corinthians 7: 1

There's a story about Michelangelo that tells a great deal about spiritual growth. He had just finished the statue of the young David, one of the most lifelike and beautiful works of art ever done. Someone is said to have asked him, "Michelangelo, how in the world did you ever do this?"

He is said to have replied, "Oh, it wasn't all that difficult. I ran across this huge stone in the quarry. And I saw David in it. Very excited, I had the stone brought back to my studio. And month after month after month, I very carefully chipped away everything that wasn't David."

That's what God did for me in my first year of the walk with Him, His Son and His Spirit.

Chip: A roller coaster of emotions and spirit. I began to fight through the denial that I truly had a problem with alcohol as the Holy Spirit convicted me to the sin.

Chip: A bit of balance, a piece of mind. I began to see that only the tremendous grace of God could save me.

Chip: New friends, a new style of life, a new way of living. I began to surrender my will to the best of my ability to God.

Chip: I began to look back at more than my drinking problem, seeing the full amount of my sin, my separation from God.

Chip: I confessed my sin to God, to myself and to another human.

Chip: I asked for forgiveness on a daily basis, seeing that I still sin, I'm still imperfect but that Jesus Christ came to forgive our sins, not condemn us for them.

Chip: I began to repair lost relationships, asking for forgiveness as a measure of restitution to my loved ones.

Chip: I was fully forgiven by all and the Holy Spirit began to teach me how to live in peace.

Chip: full-circle, back to August's searing heat. Back to the moment I began. Still sinning, but now being conscious of it, beginning to be sanctified by a loving, merciful God.

I want it clearly understood that the program of Alcoholics Anonymous is the best way, in my humble opinion, of beating a problem of alcoholic consumption. It is a spiritual program that helps hundreds of thousands daily. I believe in it as a deterrent to spiritual deadness. But the 12 steps of AA end just short of salvation.

For growing nearer to God, for your salvation, AA is incomplete. You must, I believe, take that 13th step. AA stops at the point that Jesus enters. I remind anyone reading this that Jesus is the only one who said He is the only way to the Father. No prophet, no man, no woman except Jesus made this humble boast.

For many pages I've made it clear—or tried to—that you can't save yourself from the ravages of alcohol. You can't save yourself from sin. You can't do a single thing to find lasting happiness, joy and peace.

I saved a little message for the last chapter, however.

There is ONE thing you can do. You're asked, told, required to do this. One thing. Only one.
You must believe.
That's it.
That's all.
See, for all the thousands of pages in the Bible, the thousands of pages I read in that first year in AA books, Christian books, books on spirituality, on joy, on happiness, it all comes down to one thing.
There was a man on a cross. He died. He was buried. On the third day, He arose from the dead.
It all comes down to this.
You believe it and are saved. You don't believe it, you're not. That's it.
You must believe. You won't drink again, not because it's a rule, it's against society, it might cost you your job, it might cost you your family, it might cost you your wife, it might cost you your life. It could do all these things. You won't drink because you have so much sheer gratitude bubbling up in you, so much love for the Savior, you won't disappoint Him.
You want to see Him one day, really see Him. Touch His hands, touch His cheeks, hug Him, kiss Him. You want to show Him you learned a couple of things from all that you did wrong. You want to tell him how much you love Him.
That's it. That's the answer. Simple, missed by millions in a world God still weeps over. But that's it.

✦ ✦ ✦

In the first year of sobriety, I heard so many times how people were proud of what I had done. I lapped it up like a kitten would with a bowl of milk. Eventually I began to have the chips of pride, ego, self knocked off my outer body, and my soul began to respond with love.
I did nothing but believe.

There were many, however, who did help, push, pull and love me into submission.

My wife, Mary, is the reason I was able to find help. She suffered through my alcoholism with much love. She's a special person. If God's plan is to have us be the best we can be, there are times I believe she's real close to being exactly what God had in mind. She was patient when I couldn't find a drop of patience. She was calm when I was hysterical. She was quiet when the joy of God had me up at nights talking rapidly.

She kept the family together when I was passed out. She kept the children knowing they were loved when I was such a failure.

Mary is truly an answer to a prayer.

My boss, Tim Ellerbee, is another who stood by me when I don't believe he understood what was happening to me. He and I have an unusual relationship. We're friends, even more so now than at the beginning, but—

We were also employee and employer. He contributed to a lot of the stress of the first year and is also the one person who looked after me when I put the stress on myself. I can never thank him enough. He could have treated me so much differently. Tim Ellerbee is a pleasure to know.

My new friends, my church members, my Sunday school class members, all were important. The support group you find, you must find, is critical.

What has changed? Darn near everything. Life is still what life is: never easy, never completely without stress. But I get up almost every day now ready for whatever the day will provide. I never did that before. There are still down moments, still moments when I'm so unsure where I'm supposed to go, what I'm supposed to do. Don't be fooled. You're given the key to the car, but the road map is sometimes difficult to follow.

When that happens, however I now have a method to find understanding.

And that is change.

✦ ✦ ✦

Two stories in closing:
When I was seven years old, I had a fetish for Lassie. I loved that collie. I WANTED that sable and white collie.

I went to the source of all wanting: Santa. For Christmas that year, I asked Santa for a collie, just like L-A-S-S-I-E. I was clear, articulate. To the point. There was no way for him to misunderstand. I asked for nothing else, so I didn't see it as a problem.

We went to West Virginia to visit Aunt Elsie and Uncle Jim, as we normally did.

I remember distinctly Christmas Eve. The Fairmont local television station showed a radar sighting of Santa about 9 p.m. on the Zenith black and white TV. It was a message for all the eager youngsters to get into bed.

I did, with visions of my Lassie saving me from assorted predicaments in coming years.

When I awoke, I ran down the hall into the living room. Under the tree was a brown-and-white plastic bank. A LASSIE bank. I was stunned. How could Santa have gotten this request this messed up?

When this journey began, when I began to clearly see that God was my only hope, I thought He was some sort of spiritual Santa. Ask and thou will receive, I understood.

It is neither that simple nor that complex.

You will receive. But the blessings you receive might not be the ones you had specifically asked for.

What I asked for: happiness; the chance to use all my abilities at work; health; friends.

What have I received:

A family that cares more deeply for each other than before;

A wife growing in Christ, in maturity, in leadership in her family;

A self whose pride and ego have been chipped away until whatever good is in him is finally showing through;

A life that is still filled with struggle, but which is met with peace at the end of most days.

Gifts all. I wanted greatness, thought it only diluted by alcohol. I've gotten meekness, diluted by nothing and gratefully received.

Finally, let my friend John Mark tell you a story about the very first missionary Jesus sent out. See if you, as do I, recognize an alcoholic in the message.

Jesus' ministry had begun, and he'd just calmed the storm in the lake. When Jesus and his disciples came across the lake to the region of the Garasenes, Jesus got out of the boat. What happened and Jesus' reaction to it is the reason I wrote this book.

✦ ✦ ✦

It is early morning. Jesus is rested, even energetic after a night on the lake. The disciples are tired, but strangely energized. The evening with the Lord on the lake had been quite eventful. From being sure they were going to die to becoming sure that Jesus was more than an average Galilean, their night had been far from normal.

Life with Jesus is many things, but normal is not quite one of them.

The fishing boat piloted by Peter, known to many as a very good fisherman on the lake, comes to shore at daybreak. It pulls in and Andrew is the first to leap out, pulling at the rope that will bring the boat closer for Jesus to step out in ankle-deep water. Thomas and John jump out to help.

The boat is pulled onto the shore enough that the constant ebb and flow of the water doesn't affect it.

As the tired fishermen pat each other on the backs, Jesus steps out, his dirty feet being washed clean by the surf.

He strides in as he always does, regally, in charge.

But as he does, a man rushes from the caves to their right, 100 feet from shore. These caves are used to entomb the Jewish dead. The man screams, rants, waves thickly muscled arms in the air. He's slobbering, shouting gibberish. The disciples pull back in horror. Jesus calmly stares at the figure, as the man hops into the air, lands and sprints toward the group. Blood runs down his filthy legs in streams. He's wearing old, tattered clothes and scrapes and cuts are evident all over his body.

His beard is matted, his hair disheveled. He appears to be quite the madman to the fearful disciples.

He races past Thomas, past Andrew, right up to Jesus. The disciples, taken aback, do nothing to stop the man. The bloody, bruised madman shouts in deep voice, "What do you want with me, Jesus, Son of the Most High God. Swear to God that you won't torture me."

Jesus, just the beginning of a grin on his face despite the horrific circumstances, says merely, "Come out of this man, you evil spirit!" He continues, as the man falls backward from his knees to a prone position, with, "What is your name."

Sweat is pouring off the forehead of the man. The disciples surround him, watching for a movement, waiting for the slightest indication there is danger.

The man replies, in a high-pitched whine, "My name is legion." In a scratchy, elderly female voice he sings, "For we are many." The changing voices continue, begging Jesus for pardon, begging Him not to send THEM out of the area. The disciples have seen many wonders since Jesus called them together, but nothing like this. Not remotely.

Up from the shore, as the land rises toward cliffs in the distance, is a herd of pigs. The man's many voices, sometimes one-at-a-time, sometimes together, changing word after word, beg Jesus to send them into the pigs.

Jesus ponders but a moment, waves at the pigs in a sign of permission, and suddenly the pigs are on the run. Two thousand pigs rushing down the rise toward the water. They plunge into the water, continuing to struggle until they are below the surface in a froth and swirl.

The disciples stare open-mouthed at the scene, not understanding. As usual.

Jesus pays no attention to the activity in the water.

He pays no attention as the owners of the pigs rush down the rise after their stock. They're dumbfounded about what has happened, and not the least bit happy about the turn of events.

They rush up to the man, the man they've known to be demon-filled, crazy, untouchable, unchainable, unkeepable, unsaveable. Others who have watched come rushing up. They tell the pigs' owners what they think has happened. The owners of the stock ask Jesus to leave.

It's never enough, the disciples think. Never. Jesus is always asked to leave, no matter the good he has done.

As the group wades out to the boat, a few linger to push the craft out of the shallows.

The man Jesus has healed begs him to let him go with them. "I can never repay you for what you've done for me," he shouts in a warm, loving voice. He dips his hand into the water and throws some on his face, scrubbing away debris stuck in his beard, dirt and terrible memories, thinking he can clean himself enough to be allowed to go.

He begs Jesus to allow it.

But Jesus has other plans.

"Go home to your family and tell them how much the Lord has done for you," Jesus says, "and how He has had mercy on you."

The man kisses the tender hands, backs up a step, smiles and shakes his head. He lingers as the disciples began to push the boat away from the shore. He will never see the Lord again, but he has his mission now. He will never stop telling what happened to him. Once he was lost, without hope, without a life he could be happy with, with no peace. He'd been hurting himself and his family. He'd been alone. He would never stop telling his story.

✦ ✦ ✦

It was a year I won't forget. It was a year of change, a year of study, of work and of growing love. It was a beginning. May the Holy Spirit continue to fill me, my life, my family, convicting, teaching, molding me.

I am thankful; I am blessed.

It all comes down to a man on a cross.

And His grace.

—Billy Turner, March 14, 1997